FRIENDSHIP HOMES:

If These Houses
Could Talk

Friendship Museum Inc.
P. O. Box 226
Friendship, Maine 04547
Incorporated 1964

Library of Congress # 2007926273

Friendship Homes *If These Houses Could Talk*

ISBN # 978-0-9795416-0-5 (Hardcover)
ISBN # 978-0-9795416-1-2 (Paperback)

History – United States. 2. Maine – History. 3. Friendship, Maine – History.

First Edition 2007

Designed for the Friendship Museum by Mary Ann Hensel

Project Consultant: Jane Karker, Custom Museum Publishing

Table of Contents

Acknowledgments

The publication of *Friendship Homes* is the product of a collaborative volunteer community effort in Friendship, Maine. Supported by the Friendship Museum and the Friendship Public Library, this book features the work and research of 27 volunteer writers and over 20 volunteer photographers, as well as contributions from approximately 50 different individuals and organizations. Due to the enthusiastic response from the community, a modest project of 20 chapters/homes, started in August 2006, grew to 41 chapters by the time the project concluded in 2007. Drawing from the oral history of our elders, our writers, some in their 80s and 90s, have written an informative and colorful book. Our only regret is that we were unable (time and money) to include many other homes in Friendship that certainly are equally worthy subjects.

We'd like to express our sincere appreciation to the project's benefactors. Essential financial support was provided by the Maine Community Foundation-Knox County Program and The First N.A. Additional technical support and promotional material were generously provided by the *Maine Antique Digest*. Without the support of these organizations, this project would not have been possible.

With so many individuals and organizations to thank, it's difficult to decide where to begin. Perhaps it's appropriate to first thank our forebears, whose lives and stories came to light in this book. In the 18th century, Meduncook Plantation suffered the ravages of frontier warfare during the French and Indian Wars and later contributed soldiers to the American Revolution. Given Maine's importance in the nation's history in the 19th century, perhaps we shouldn't have been surprised to discover so many men and women of incredible stature. While this book project began as a limited history of selected homes in Friendship, it is the stories these homes tell about the people of Friendship that brought the project to life. Here we find Sea Ledge, the first seasonal cottage on Davis Point built by Warren's Civil War hero, General Ellis Spear. Friendship also had its own authentic Civil War hero, Sergeant Melville B. Cook. Enlisting on September 26, 1861, Cook was the first man from Friendship to join the Union's cause. Wounded three times, once seriously, Cook continued to serve in a variety of battles until the end of the war in 1865. Just take one look at Melville Cook's picture in chapter 9 of this book — solid is the word that comes to mind — a perfect example of the character of Friendship's people and their history. We think you'll agree that Friendship was full of interesting characters, men and women, who contributed to their town and country. We hope you enjoy their stories as much as we did in discovering their histories.

We would like to thank our 27 volunteer writers for their time and research. Our sincere gratitude goes to: Priscilla Ambrose, Barbara Beebe, Alice Benner, Celia Lash Briggs, Linda Sylvester DeRosa, David Edwards, Ann Martin Filippi, Carolyn Foster, Walter Foster, David Adams Hovell, Liga V. Jahnke, Eleanor Cook Lang, Marilyn Lash, Joseph Lebherz, Kathy MacLeod, Nancy Bellhouse May, Lynn Meyer, Bonnie Davis Micue, Julie Spear Pugh, Cicely Aikman Scherer, James E. and Nina M. Scott, Eliza Soeth, Marguerite Sylvester, Mary Flood Thompson, Mike J. Trigilio, and Patricia Winchenbach.

In the course of writing this book, we received much editorial help and many constructive comments from a talented core of volunteers. We owe a great debt to Carolyn Foster, Chip and Liga Jahnke, Marguerite C. Sylvester, Alana and Gerritt VanDerwerker, and Patricia Winchenbach.

The project also utilized the talents of over 20 volunteer photographers, who produced work far beyond our expectations. Thanks to Celia L. Briggs, Elizabeth K. Bunbury, Adolfo Chavez III, Terry L. Clinch, Warren Conary, Bill Cook, Elaine Lang Cornett, Robert Cornett, Linda S. DeRosa, Jed Devine, Walter Foster, Margaret Wotton Gagnon, James C. Hensel, Carol Hoch, Polly Jones, Susan Lott, Amy McCollett, Kathy MacLeod, Kenneth MacLeod, Arthur K. McFarland, Victor Motyka, William Olsen, Jack Pugh, Fran Richardson, Eliza Soeth, Chuck Thompson, Michael J. Trigilio, Gordon Winchenbach, Pat Winchenbach, and Gary P. Zientara.

The project received valuable technical assistance, background historical information, old photographs, and advice from a variety of sources. We want to thank each of you who devoted time to make this a better project: Becky Benner, Stephen Burns, Jim Flagg, Walter Foster, Margaret Wotton Gagnon, Patricia Jameson Havener, Kevin Johnson, Robert Lash Jr., Amy McCollett, Tim McLaughlin, Wanda Smith, Arlene Stetson, Gordon Winchenbach, Harolyn York, and an anonymous conservator.

The project utilized the talents of many artists, past and present, to accent this book. We would like to acknowledge each of their contributions: Barbara Beebe, Sam Cady, Kerr Eby, Celia Hensel, Steve Hensel, Katharina Keoughan, Clinton Lawry I, Helene F. McGorrill, Maude Olsen, George F. Payne, Marion Powers (Kirkpatrick), Arthur P. Spear, William P. Stubbs, and Sherman Wotton.

Thanks also go to the Maine Historic Preservation Commission and to Director Earle G. Shettleworth Jr., who wrote the superb introduction for this book. Thanks also to Christi Mitchell, the Architectural Historian at the Commission, for her time and help.

We would also like to thank Les Fossel of Restoration Resources, who agreed to headline our project fund-raiser dinner and who put on a great presentation about older New England homes. Those in attendance really enjoyed his program.

We also would like to express our gratitude to Custom Museum Publishing of Rockland, Maine, and to its owner, Jane Karker. Jane patiently worked and guided our volunteer process forward. It was a pleasure to work with her in bringing our project to fruition.

We also owe debts of gratitude to the Friendship Museum and the Friendship Public Library, the two organizations that sponsored this project. Special thanks are due to Celia Briggs, Friendship's librarian and the project's coordinator; Mary Ann Hensel, project designer and computer expert; Linda DeRosa, chief liaison officer, and Jeffrey Evangelos, the business manager. Without their tireless efforts, this project would not have been possible.

We apologize if we have inadvertently omitted anyone from this list. Scores of people have supported this effort, and our gratitude goes out to all of you.

Looking west toward Friendship Harbor.   *Photo by Gary P. Zientara*

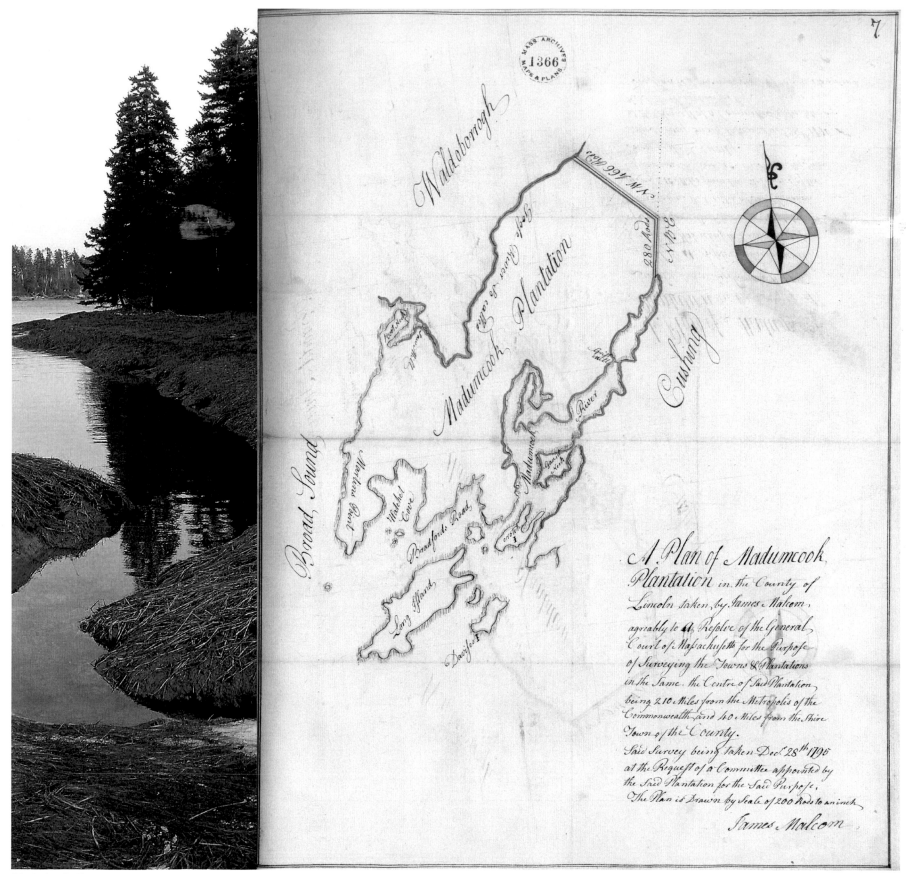

Introduction

There are many ways to relate the history of a town. A common device is to present a chronology of names, dates, and events; albeit, this is rudimentary and lacks the depth of causality and connection. Charting a town's economic or cultural booms and busts opens the discourse somewhat but can lead to value judgments on the relative worth of any particular era. Analysis of settlement patterns and architectural styles provides more tangible links to historical moments and human movements, but these, too, are all but mute if the context of their development is ignored. While each of these is an element of "the history" of a place, it is the people who gave and give a community life. Histories are not compiled solely for the sake of events long past, businesses shuttered, or houses erected; they are created to explain how our towns evolved to become the places we inhabit. At the base of historic inquiry is a desire to learn about the people of the past. The present volume is rich in people, and it is their experiences that help to create a holistic history of Friendship, Maine.

Yet the stories related here did not happen in a vacuum, and I recommend reading *Friendship Homes: If These Houses Could Talk* with a detailed map at hand. The stories are linked to houses and neighborhoods, to coves and harbors, to schools and wharfs. The stories travel from the shores of Friendship to the islands and shoals, down the coast, and into Portland and Boston and New York. The stories trace the people of Friendship at war, out west, and in distant ports. And as the residents of Friendship interacted with the world, so too did the world influence the residents of Friendship. An essential reason we study local history beyond genealogy and antiquarianism is that the history of each town in Maine is an essential piece of the greater puzzle and helps to illustrate broader historical themes. Local events reflect broad aspects of state and national history even as they create these patterns through culture, politics, and industry. It is by examining these connections, as reflected in these stories and manifest on this landscape, that a more complete understanding of Friendship will emerge.

Between 1783 and 1826, 226 new towns in Maine were incorporated, more than five times as many as had existed before. For many years a whimsical signpost in Friendship has related the distinctive names and distances to neighboring towns: "Freedom 45, Liberty 33, Harmony 96, Unity 52, Union 20, Hope 27," finishing aptly enough that "Friendship is here!" As they incorporated, each of these towns chose names that expressed and, if the truth be told, advertised an attribute that the residents felt represented the character of their town. With the exception of Union, which chose its name in 1786, and Liberty, which seceded from Montville in 1827, these towns all incorporated and chose their names between 1803 and 1813. During this period, the towns were emerging from their adolescence and starting to define themselves as distinct places. At the same time, however, the western counties of New York and the newly designated Northwest Territories (Ohio, Michigan,

Wisconsin, Illinois, and Indiana) were luring families away from the East Coast. The future and success of any new town in Maine was dependent on attracting stable families and building the community. Each of the new Maine towns was competing for new residents, and the appellations they chose certainly helped to project a positive image. In this context, the appeal of place names evoking friendship, unity, and hope is even more appropriate. In 1800 Friendship contained a population of 330; ten years later the numbers had increased by 144; and twenty years later the tally stood at 587.

Nevertheless, the incorporation of Friendship in 1807 was not its beginning. That occurred over a period six decades earlier. In comparison to the older, established, and crowded southern New England towns, especially those on the shore north of Boston, the eastern frontier of Massachusetts was sparsely populated by colonists and other Europeans. (It has been estimated that Maine was inhabited by about 29,000 white persons on the eve of the Revolution.) Maine was full of timber, a scarce commodity in the older colonies and in England, but without a population to fell the forests, the area was also less than profitable and subject to instability. By opening Maine lands to settlers, the General Court of Massachusetts hoped to accomplish several goals simultaneously: relieve the overcrowding in the south, provide more opportunities for people to own land, cement Massachusetts's political control over the area, and establish a density and permanence of population that would discourage conflict with the Native Americans who lived in the eastern frontier. In order to obtain this goal, the General Court offered groups of residents either townships or affirmed the validity of royal patents made by the English Crown in the seventeenth century.

The Muscongus Patent (originally granted in 1630 and later better known as the Waldo Patent) contained a million acres between the Medomak River and Penobscot Bay, and by 1735 it was under the control of Samuel Waldo, the majority stakeholder. In order to capitalize on the natural resources found thereon (mostly lumber), it was imperative that Waldo establish lasting settlements. To do this he started to offer groups of settlers incentives to relocate to coastal Maine. Starting in 1735 he brought Scots-Irish families to Warren and later to Thomaston. In 1742, 1751, and 1753 he brought German immigrants to Waldoboro. On the peninsula that is now Friendship, Waldo established the Meduncook Plantation and on its rocky coast settled twenty families or so from southern New England. Nevertheless, mid-eighteenth-century settlement in Lincoln (later Knox) County was not a straightforward affair. It is important to remember that often multiple parties claimed the same lands, and in many cases it was difficult to establish a solid title to any piece of land. Even the royal patents and land grants from the General Court were subject to poor surveys and conflicting claimants; and long before European settlers had reached the Maine coast, its Native American population had been living there on the abundance and accessibility of marine resources. The 1758 confrontation between Meduncook settlers and the Abenaki, in which several members of the Bradford family perished, was emblematic of the contest for control of the Maine lands that was occurring at many levels throughout the region.

Although the general perception is that the early coastal residents initially claimed these islands, harbors, and coves because they desired the best fishing grounds, this is, at least in part, a misconception. Overwhelmingly, the new immigrants had been farmers in Massachusetts, and after five generations of growth in their home towns, there was little land left for them to work. It was only after they realized that the coastal Maine land was rocky and infertile that they turned to fishing in great numbers. At first this was to provide sustenance and some trade; eventually maritime pursuits came to define coastal communities.

Among the saltwater farms in Friendship was that of Jesse Thomas, Senior and Junior. The 1776 Des Barres chart of the Meduncook area clearly shows the boundaries of the cleared fields behind their homestead. Other large farms depicted on this map were in the vicinity of William Condon's property on Condon Head, later the same neighborhood in which James and Hannah Condon kept their oxen, cows, and sheep and the Pottles raised chickens and vegetables in the twentieth century. Of the roughly 46 houses shown on this map, the vast majority were positioned on the headlands above the Meduncook and Little Rivers. Fewer properties were situated in close proximity to the water, just above the tidal plain. Productive farming was essential for the survival of any new community, and even as late as 1850, seventy-five of the 196 adult men in town identified themselves as farmers, but even those settlers who persisted in agricultural endeavors often supplemented their incomes with maritime activities.

Even a casual glance at this volume reveals the extent to which the sea has been an important partner in the life of the town. Extrapolating beyond Friendship's boundaries, this has also been the case for the state as a whole. Shaped by glaciers during the last ice age, the state's 2,500 mile coastline and long, navigable inland waterways provided the direction for Maine's growth and were intimately linked to the development of its communities. Three interconnected activities, namely maritime commerce, fishing, and shipbuilding, provided the means for the development not only of towns like Friendship, but the state as a whole.

One of the most visible and lasting symbols of the maritime heritage found on the coast of Maine are her numerous light stations and lighthouses. Their picturesque appeal aside, Maine's light stations had assumed important roles in establishing the state's critical maritime transportation network since the first station was erected in the state in 1790. Prominently located at strategic offshore, coastal, and river sites, they were constructed, at first, in response to specific local needs, but later they were a part of a coast-wide pattern of aids to navigation that was a key component in enabling the growth of the maritime trade. They were designed to provide both distantly visible directional land-

marks to specific coastal areas as well as warning signals to various hazards. From coasting vessels to large schooners, pinkies to steamships, they functioned to help safely and efficiently guide vessels into harbors and around ledges. The immense tonnage of raw and finished products, including lumber, fish, granite, ice, lime, and brick that was shipped from the state's numerous seaports testifies at once to the need for and the ultimate success of the system of navigational aids that greatly facilitated commercial maritime transportation.

From 1807 on, the Franklin Island Light keepers and their families were entrusted with keeping the beacons lit and played an important part in enabling the commercial growth of the entire state. That they realized the interconnectedness and importance of their vocation probably buffeted them against the harsh weather, continuous work, and physical isolation that so often characterized their lives.

As this volume relates, among the vessels that passed the Franklin Light were those of Friendship's master mariners. For men like N. Webb Thompson and Fernando Francis and their families, passing the light station set them upon voyages of trade to ports throughout the world. Upon their return, they brought not only the profits or loss of their enterprise but an expanded world experience that radiated through their families, neighborhoods, and towns. Mary Ellen Chase, who grew up in Blue Hill at the turn of the twentieth century, reflected on the effect that these voyages had on the trajectory of the entire community:

> "...to have been born at a time when great ships,
> built by Maine people in a hundred seacoast villages,
> had been for nearly a century making Searsport and
> Rockland, Belfast and Thomaston, Wiscasset and
> Calais better known in Canton, Singapore, and Sydney
> than even New York and London were known; to have
> been brought up with men, and with women, too, who
> knew the Seven Seas too well to be bounded in their
> thoughts by the narrow confines of their own native
> parishes; - such an inheritance of imperishable values
> imposes a debt which cannot possibly either be under-
> estimated or ever fully discharged."[1]

In the holds of these vessels were the products of the international market. Yet so, too, did the lighthouse function for the Grand Banks or inshore fishermen whose work took them away from town for weeks or hours rather than years. The history of Maine fishing is the subject of many volumes, and from the seventeenth century to the present it has played an important role in Maine's coastal communities. The first European visitors to North America were following large schools of cod, and the economic benefits derived from harvesting this resource was an important catalyst in the European colonization of the continent. Fishing stations subsequently sprang up in Pemaquid and Cape

1. Colby Library Quarterly Series VI, No.1 March 1962, Waterville, Me. *from The Diamond Jubilee of Mary Ellen Chase, edited by Eleanor S. Duckett et al. My Novels About Maine, by Mary Ellen Chase* pp. 14-15.

Newagen and on Monhegan and Damariscove Islands. Well into the first quarter of the eighteenth century fish was the principal staple export from Maine, and through the nineteenth century most of the cod was dried and salted ashore and then shipped to ports from Europe to South America as well as to ports up and down the East Coast.

The separation in 1820 of Maine from Massachusetts and its admission to the Union coincided with the beginning of a period of growth that reinforced the significance of the state's maritime resources. In the period 1820 -1826 the total output of the fishing industry in the United States averaged 63,987 tons per year. Maine's share totaled 12,326 tons per year or nearly twenty percent of the total. By the census of 1860, nearly one in five residents of the state was a mariner, and at that time in Friendship most of the mariners fished for cod. Indeed, in 1860 the Maine Products of Industry census identified 27 men in Friendship as cod fishermen. They owned 26 vessels and employed seventy additional workers in harvesting, salting, or curing cod. Hake and mackerel were also caught and sold in lesser quantities. The offshore cod industry waned quickly after the Civil War, but the large wharf where the Morse family processed their cod reminds us of the former scale of this industry in Friendship.

Even as offshore ground fishing became less profitable, there rose a new market for an abundant Maine product, lobster; and correspondingly the 1870 census recorded a rise among the residents of Friendship who identified themselves as lobstermen. Initially the lobsters trapped along the Maine coast were loaded into out-of-state lobster smacks and transported to markets in Boston and New York. After the Civil War most of the lobster smacks that plied Friendship's waters were providing lobster for the canning factories in Boothbay and other nearby ports. Although Friendship never had a lobster cannery, it was directly affected by the tremendous explosion in the demand for lobster that occurred after the first canneries opened. In Maine, according to one account, "The number of lobstermen exploded, from a few dozen in the late 1840s to 1,843 in 1880."[2]

For over 150 years, the waters around Friendship have been continually fished for lobster, and this longevity is due in part to the localized nature of the fishing grounds and the regional conservatism that governs both regulatory and cultural attitudes toward the industry. In Friendship the contribution of Randall Condon, who pressed the state legislature in 1887 to establish legal size limits, is not to be underestimated. Nor do townspeople forget that in 1916 the first lobstering license granted in the state went to local resident Charles Murphy. Although the nature of this coastal industry has changed over the years, catching lobsters is the most lucrative and culturally important industry for Friendship. Those who were not setting lobster pots were building the Friendship sloops that enabled the lobstermen to navigate and fish the local waters so deftly.

For every family that historically made its living fully or partially from the sea, there was a vessel that took them past the Franklin Island Light Station. Beginning in the early decades of the seventeenth century, the abundance and variety of timber, coupled with the deep sheltered waterways, encouraged the development of local shipbuilding, albeit on a small scale. Throughout Maine, shipbuilding gained momentum in the 1820s, when for the first time its production exceeded that of Massachusetts; and in the following decade it surpassed New York and Massachusetts combined, thereby leading the United States. By 1855, the peak of Maine's "Golden Age of the Wooden Ship," 215,904 tons of shipping capacity were built in its yards, which was more than one-third of the total production in the United States. The plentiful timber resources, combined with local ingenuity and a firsthand knowledge of the sea, enabled boat builders to produce a significant variety of Maine-built vessels. Among the best known of these were the multi-masted schooners out of Bath, Waldoboro, and Camden, and the Downeast clippers from Searsport, Damariscotta, and Phippsburg. Although the Friendship peninsula was not particularly rich in timber, a shipbuilding industry developed nonetheless. According to one estimate, fourteen schooners or other oceangoing fishing vessels were built in town between 1830 and 1880. As the lobster industry started to become profitable, local builders produced between 25 and 30 lobster smacks between 1865 and 1880, but it is the Friendship sloop, an adroit vessel ideal for navigating coastal waters, that has garnered the most notoriety for the region. Although the first designer of this vessel type has not been positively established, Wilbur A. Morse was certainly the most prolific builder of Friendship sloops, turning out nine sloops in the year 1900 alone. Now entirely replaced by motorized lobster boats, these sloops offered an ideal carriage in which to work the inshore waters.

As noted earlier, agriculture was important in communities like Friendship and throughout the state. A symbol of this is found on the state seal, which depicts both a husbandman and a mariner. Agricultural census figures reveal that in terms of the number of farms, improved acreage, and numbers of livestock, farming in Maine reached its zenith in 1880 notwithstanding the development of the potato-growing lands of Aroostook County. From this point forward, the agricultural landscape in the older settled parts of the state began to undergo a dramatic transformation and decline. Many factors were responsible for this: formerly productive fields were overworked and stripped of their fertility; employment opportunities expanded in the urban areas; and there was a steady decline in prices for farm products. In addition, better agricultural lands were opened for settlement in the Midwest and West, and within as few as three generations from settlement in some sections of the state, young families headed west to try their hands at prairie farming or were lured away to work in railroad towns or in the gold fields, like

2. Colin Woodward, *The Lobster Coast: Rebels, Rusticators, and the Struggle for a Forgotten Frontier* (New York: Viking, 2004), P.186.

William T. Thomas. Already identified as a miner in the 1860 Friendship census (even before he left town), William met considerable financial success in Eureka, California, a port town filled with miners, loggers, and fishermen, before moving on to the mines in Nevada City. Others, such as Melville Bradford Cook and the Jameson boys, left Maine to serve in the Civil War. All but eight of the 83 men who enlisted from Friendship lived through the conflict, and many returned. The words of Jonah Jameson, "I should like to be at home..." remind us that although the lure of duty and patriotism was strong, and the desire to "put down this wicked Rebellion which is now ravaging in the land" was just, the men who ventured thus kept thoughts of home and family close at hand.

Those who remained in Maine in the second half of the nineteenth century increasingly obtained employment in newly emerging industries, including textiles, lime, granite, ice, lumber, and canned products. A brief passage in the chapter on the Fred Young House hints at one industry through which Friendship was represented beyond its borders.

In explaining the erection of the two-story ell on the back of the Greek Revival style cape built by Fred Bradford, the author reflects that the ell was used "as a boarding house for workers in the Long Island granite quarries" prior to 1900. According to C. William Vogel's, *History of Friendship*, quarrying on Friendship Long Island occurred during the last quarter of the century. The Union Granite Company specialized in "stone for monumental works, perhaps the most famous was the supply of granite for Grant's Tomb in New York."[3] As many as 125 men were employed by the company, which in 1895 was one of 153 such operations in the state. In addition to monumental and sculptural stone, Maine's granite works also produced curbstones, paving stones, and structural blocks. The quality of the granite was known far and wide. With only a few exceptions, the quarries were located in close proximity to the water — both because that was where the thin soil over the stone was easiest to work but also to facilitate shipping the stone by large ships. Indeed, in 1889 the Union Granite Co. built a large wharf on Friendship Long Island at which the vessels could dock. The quarry operation also contained a blacksmith's shop, a steam engine and train shed, a machine shop, cutting sheds, office building, cook house, store, and boarding house. Italians and Scandinavians worked alongside Friendship natives at the quarry, and while many lived on the island, others boarded at mainland establishments such as the house that Fred Bradford owned.

Canneries were another industry that rose to prominence during the nineteenth century and exported the resources of Maine's towns far beyond their borders. Although rudimentary canning techniques were introduced in France in 1809, it took several decades for the process to be perfected and to travel to the United States. Portland, the "pioneering center of canning," had its first corn cannery in 1840, and lobster was canned 10 years later.[4] Through the Civil War, canned goods provided needed sus-

Dory on a mooring in Blackfish Cove.   *Photo by Cecily Davey Havener*

tenance on the front lines, and in the decades that followed the industry continued to grow. To corn and lobster were added sardines and mackerel, herring, and beef. The cannery operators' attention turned to clams about 1875. With its wide clam flats in Hatchet Cove, residents of Friendship had, like Charlie Murphy, been harvesting the bivalves for bait for many years. When Burnham and Morrill, one of the largest canning companies in the state, opened its clam factory on the wharf, they offered employment for residents like Ivernia Wallace and her neighbors. Similarly, the residents of Friendship participated in the ice trade for a few decades around the turn of the century, although as David Adams Hovell points out, the success of this venture was probably curtailed by the propensity for the ice to contain bits of vegetation from the pond!

In addition to the heavy volume of merchant traffic that passed up and down the coast, steam passenger vessels connected the coastal and larger river towns with urban areas such as Portland, Boston, and New York. Before automobiles were invented and roads improved to serve them, the steamers that docked at Jameson and Wotton's wharf opened the coastal communities. Among the passengers on these vessels were those who came not on business but for pleasure. These urban travelers first spotted the harbor towns as they journeyed toward developing resort areas, and many took note of the fine vistas and tidy houses. The seemingly quiet, pristine, and rural landscape appealed to their growing desire to escape the crowded and unhealthy urban neighborhoods, at least for a few of the hottest months each year. Eventually, these passengers disembarked at ports up and down the coast, and the phenomenon of the summer people was born.

Not all of the folks who established summer homes were from

3. William Vogel, *History of Friendship* (Orono, Maine:University of Maine), p.10.
4. W. H. Bunting, *A Day's Work* (Gardiner, Maine: Tilbury House, Publishers, 1997), p.228.

away. As the story of the Samuel Lawry House and others remind us, ancestral homesteads were retained by relocated family members who returned annually to reconnect with their roots. Others were like the Warren native General Ellis Spear, who chose a spot near relatives on Davis Point on which to build his cottage. Whether the summer people came from afar or just over the county line, they brought with them elements of the world beyond and the town became dotted with hotels and guest houses, new architecture, and amenities such as bowling alleys. These waterfront homes and cottages differed from the saltwater farms and homes of the established families in town at the Corner, in their scale, design, and functionality; they were planned to enhance relaxation and recreation rather than to shelter a working family. Although it would initially seem that the summer people and Friendship natives lived in two different worlds, over the decades the lines have blurred as families intermarried and some summer homes were converted to year-round residences. Today, many newer residents carefully and respectfully preserve and retain the stories, traditions, and buildings of the town's past even as they add their voices to the town's future.

As the world has evolved and the faces have changed over the seasons, decades, and centuries, in many ways Friendship has clung to its roots. Tight family connections, strong community ties, and an economy strengthened by fishing and farming still characterize this harbor town. After two hundred years of exporting its products and people and importing new products and people, one constant remains — Friendship is here!

Earle G. Shettleworth, Jr.
State Historian

Friendship is here.

Photo by Linda S. DeRosa

I | Island Homes

Keepers of Franklin Light

Thomas Hanna (c. 1830s)
James Hanna (c. 1840s)
William Jameson (c. 1845)
Edward Thomas (c. 1845)
William Blasdel (1850–1854)
Peter Williams (1855)
James W. Farrow (1859–1871)
Charles A. Dolliver (1871–1884)
Frank W. Whitney (1884–1888)
George D. Pottle (1888–1900)
Edward T. Spurling (1900–1911)
Eugene N. Larrabee (1911)
Almon Mitchell (1911–1913)
Albert J. Clinch (1913–1918)
Vinal O. Beal (1918–1919)
Roscoe Chandler (1919–1924)
George Woodward (1924–1926)
Charles N. Robinson (1926–1933)

Photo by Arthur K. McFarland, Jr.

1 *Franklin Island Light* By Joseph Lebherz

In the early 19th century, shipping was the main source of transportation along the coast of Maine. Trade was at an all time high in the vicinity of Muscongus Bay and the St. George River. As trade increased, the loss of ships and lives in the area of Franklin Island also increased. The need for a lighthouse was obvious.

On June 24, 1806, under President Thomas Jefferson, an act was passed to build a lighthouse on Franklin Island.

Franklin Light.   Photo by Terry L. Clinch

Inclement weather and the lack of building materials delayed the completion of the octagonal wooden tower and dwelling until 1807. With completion of the tower, the light of 10 lamps with 14" reflectors was visible for 12 nautical miles. This was quite impressive for an early light, the third to be constructed on the Maine coast. It served as a guide to three rivers, the St. George, the Meduncook, and the Medomak. The tower, as we see it today, was rebuilt in 1855 with brick, and included the installation of a fourth order Fresnel lens. Lard oil was used for the light until 1875. In coldest weather the light keeper had to run a small fire in the tower to keep the lard from congealing. A wooden dwelling was also erected. There was pastureland for a cow and a few sheep, a good garden spot, and water was collected in a cistern from rainfall.

The tower still stands today, although the keeper's dwelling and other structures, with the exception of the oil house, were taken down about 1937. Byron Burns, a Friendship lobster fisher-

George and Arvilla Pottle.
Photo courtesy of Gordon and Pat Winchenbach

man told his son Stephen, that a crew from the government tore down the keeper's house during the Depression, stacked the lumber neatly in piles, and then burned the piles. Byron thought

Keeper Albert J. Clinch family.   *Photo courtesy of Terry L. Clinch*

that the lumber could have been offered to fishermen who wanted to build camps on the islands.[1]

Little is known about the lives of the keepers with the exception of a few. George Pottle became keeper of the light in 1888, remaining there until 1900. During his tenure as a keeper, a near disaster was avoided one foggy morning. A two-masted lime coaster under the command of Captain Hart of Thomaston came perilously near the rocks on the wrong side of the light. In fact Capt. Hart was so close he was able to hold a conversation from ship to shore without any difficulty.[2] Being warned of danger by Mr. Pottle, he was able to divert his course away from the hazards. The Pottle family had increased in size by one, with the birth of their youngest son, Willie, while on the island. In 1900 they moved to Martin Point Road on the mainland. The Pottle home is now owned by his great-grandson Gordon Winchenbach and his wife, Patricia.

Albert James Clinch was appointed to the Franklin Island Light on April 29, 1913, earning an annual salary of $600.00 until January 1, 1917, when his salary was increased to $648.00 for a year's service. Mr. Clinch served at the Halfway Rock Light Station in Casco Bay, Maine as first assistant keeper before receiving his appointment to the Muscongus Bay area. He brought his wife, Tirzah Emery Purington Clinch, and four children to the island, spending six years, nine months, and three days on Franklin.[3]

The first peril the family had to overcome was disembarking from the sailing vessel by

Ornate tower staircase.   *Photo courtesy of Terry L. Clinch*

Postcard of Franklin Light, circa 1900.

Courtesy of Marguerite C. Sylvester

INSTRUCTIONS

TO THE KEEPERS OF LIGHT-HOUSES WITHIN THE UNITED STATES.

1. You are to light the lamps every evening at sun-setting, and keep them continually burning, bright and clear, till sun-rising.

2. You are to be careful that the lamps, reflectors, and lanterns, are constantly kept clear, and in order; and particularly to be careful that no lamps, wood, or candles, be left burning any where so as to endanger fire.

3. In order to maintain the greatest degree of light during the night, the wicks are to be trimmed every four hours, taking care that they are exactly even on the top.

4. You are to keep an exact account of the quantity of oil received from time to time; the number of gallons, quarts, gills, &c., consumed each night; and deliver a copy of the same to the Superintendent every three months, ending 31 March, 30 June, 30 September, and 31 December, in each year; with an account of the quantity on hand at the time.

5. You are not to sell, or permit to be sold, any spirituous liquors on the premises of the United States; but will treat with civility and attention, such strangers as may visit the Light-house under your charge, and as may conduct themselves in an orderly manner.

6. Should the Superintendent omit to supply the quantity of oil, wicks, tube-glasses, or other articles necessary to keep the lights in continual operation, you will give him timely notice thereof, that he may forward the requisite supplies.

7. You will not absent yourself from the Light-house, at any time, without first obtaining the consent of the Superintendent, unless the occasion be so sudden and urgent as not to admit of an application to that officer; in which case, by leaving a suitable substitute, you may be absent for twenty-four hours.

8. All your communications intended for this office, must be transmitted through the Superintendent; through whom the proper answer will be returned.

Fifth Auditor and Acting Commissioner of the Revenue.

TREASURY DEPARTMENT,
FIFTH AUDITOR'S OFFICE.

climbing down a rope ladder into a small boat that was most likely bouncing around in wind-blown waves. The Clinch family oral history states that Tirzah was "scared to death" never having had the chance to practice this agility test. During Mr. Clinch's years of service on the island, two more children were born. The first was born on May 20, 1914, and was named for his birthplace, Franklin I. Clinch. A sister, Lola, was also island born on April 20, 1916.

On record is the story of Mr. Clinch's timely rescue of Mr. William Collamore, whose boat had experienced an engine failure. Mr. Clinch was returning from a trip to Round Pond and noticed Mr. Collamore adrift. He towed Mr. Collamore to Wreck Island where he was camping, thereby averting a more serious problem.

In 1924-1926 George Woodward was the keeper. His son, Coleman, acted as assistant when needed. He recalls that summers on Franklin Island were spent partly on the boat that the Lighthouse Service furnished. It was a lapstrake dory with nothing but oars, and it was a six-mile trip to Friendship where supplies were to be purchased. On Franklin Island you didn't send messages back and forth. If you needed assistance, you were to fly the American flag upside down from the top of the tower. The only time his father had to resort to that was when he was sick with the flu. The flag was flown for two and a half days and was not seen. By then he had recovered.

In 2007 those lighthouse/lightkeeper days seem nostalgic, intriguing, and even inviting, but to those who lived that life, it was a harsh, hard-working, little-paying, lonely life and oftentimes filled with danger.

In 1967, the lighthouse was automated and its Fresnel lens removed. The tower now stands as an active aid to navigation.

Postcard of Franklin Light, circa 1890s.

Courtesy of Friendship Museum collection

2 *Captain James Simmons — "Lettie's House"* By Barbara Beebe

Lettie's House had stood empty for more than twenty years when I bought it in 1985 from Lettie's niece, Geneva Pierce. Local legend tells of the house being haunted. Years without a resident had taken its toll. The exterior ell walls were patched with tarpaper, and the rose canes and lilac bushes had crept against the walls and ell door, seeking entrance. The roof leaked and one of the chimneys was gone, having been struck by lightning. A raccoon lived in an easy chair in the parlor.

I was told when I purchased Lettie's House that it had been built about the time of the American Civil War (1861-1865). The earliest newspapers found under the parlor carpeting are dated June 30, 1877. The house was most likely built by Lettie's father, James Simmons, Jr., and Lettie was probably born in this house.

Lettie Rosetta Simmons Collamore (1881-1968) was the youngest daughter of James Simmons, Jr. (1835-1923) and his wife, Emily (Davis) Simmons, (1840-1910), and the last of their family of seven or eight children to live in the house that became known as Lettie's House. In *Chronicles of Cushing and Friendship*, the family is listed, with their ages, under the Population of Friendship, May 1892: James Simmons 57, Emily (Davis) his wife 51, Mary H 30, Roscoe E 25, C Albert 22, Emma L 20, Eugene W 16, Lulu B 14, Lettie R 10. Ivan Morse, in his published oral history, *Friendship Long Island*, says that another son, Milton, died when he was 14 or 15 years old.[1]

Lettie Simmons Collamore.

Photo courtesy of Ralph Copeland

Lettie kept the island's only post office, (1916-1922), rowing her dory to the mainland to collect the island mail. The post office was first kept in her father's general store located on Lobster Gut. He had bought the store from Mr. Trowbridge, the former boss at the Union Granite Quarry on the island.[2] Crates from this store which sold, among other things, men's boots, calico, and sugar – "the essential food" – were found and remain in Lettie's House. Lettie's father, Jim Simmons, was shot with buckshot in the neck, face, and tongue in the woods on the island by a schoolboy, who supposedly intended to rob him. Although he lived, his speech was slurred. Lettie could understand him, helped him in the store, and generally took care of him until he died in 1923.[3]

In 1925 Lettie, aged 44, married Nelson Collamore (1872-1935), age 53. According to Ivan Morse's book, Lettie and Nelson ran a farm at Lettie's House. According to Ivan Morse, Lettie did most of the work, while Nelson told her what to do. They raised vegetables for sale to the summer colony, kept a cow and some hens, and burnt over some of Jim's pasture to raise blueberries to sell.[4] Lettie used her .22 rifle to scare seagulls away from her blueberries.

Lettie and Nelson had no children and Nelson died ten years after their marriage. Over the years Lettie traded land for work done, sold off other land, and gave away strips and pieces. She lived her last years on the mainland in Friendship with her sister Emma, always hoping to be able to return to the island. She died in 1968 without realizing her dream and is buried in Friendship's Harbor Cemetery.

When my daughter, Susan Beebe, and I moved into Lettie's House on May 7, 1985, as active artists in pursuit of our craft, we were filled with the anticipation of capturing the natural beauty that encompassed this homestead. Paths entered the property from every direction, seemingly making the location a hub. One climbed up from Lobster Gut to the high spot

Emily Davis Simmons and three daughters.

Photo courtesy of Marguerite C. Sylvester

Island House with Lupines, 17" x 14" gouache painting, 1995, by Barbara Beebe

With permission of Bayberry Press, Thomaston, Maine

where we were located. Another quietly crept out of the woods from the southwest, and a major walking path passed from north to south right by the kitchen windows. In the fall of 1985 when we once again painted the new clapboards white, the house began to look solid, square, and secure.

We saw then how pretty the rooms would be. The rooms were well thought out and the house well built. We decided to take on all of the interior restoration ourselves. No structural changes were made. The homemade couch of crates, laths, and quilts is still a prominent feature in the kitchen. The large woodbox still serves to hold firewood. Two dry sinks are used for washing up and for holding pails of well water. Good pine flooring was discovered beneath the worn linoleum. Old wallpaper was removed, new applied. Little did we imagine it would take us ten years to complete this labor of love.

For three complete winters we survived in Lettie's House as year-round residents. In 2001 my daughter married and moved to the mainland. Presently, I live in the house for ten months each year much in the same way as the earlier dwellers did. I cook on the wood-burning "Wood Bishop, Acadia B. No. 89, 1885" kitchen stove. It has a magic oven – the door opens by itself when it is hot enough to bake. Dropping a pail in the original hand-dug, rock-lined well and bringing it up the hill bucketful by bucketful is how I get my water. Butter, cheese and wine keep well in the cool cellar with its quarried granite foundation. Fresh eggs are gathered daily from my chickens. Candlelight is the light used for reading at night. The old-fashioned outhouse is still in use.

The lilac planted near the front door when the house was built still thrives and blooms in late May. The original central trunks are thick and gnarled, and the lilac now sprawls into a thicket as big as the house. Among other old plants we found growing there is an early variety of delphinium, "Belladonna," 1890. Sky blue with a "bee," it blooms each July between the two east-facing kitchen windows and attracts the returning hummingbirds. In June the large east meadow blooms with the escaped garden lupine in blue, pink, and white. A *Rosa rugosa* thicket hosts a catbird's nest every summer. When walking up the path from Lobster Gut, I am often serenaded with catbird calls and a flash of charcoal grey. Canada geese appear to use the house as a migratory landmark each fall and spring, and why not? Lettie's House has stood there for more than a century and is clearly visible from the sky.

Lettie's House has been restored to a happy productive island home.

In the more than twenty years I have lived here, it has been an especially creative place. The beauty, simplicity of life, isolation, and independence I experience here on Friendship Long Island makes me create.[5] Within this protective serenity, Susan and I have produced paintings, illustrations, jewelry, and a toy theatre – built in one of the old store crates, from which a Beebe-written play of *Cinderella* was produced for island children and their parents.[6]

The ghost that haunted "Lettie's House" has not been seen or heard since one bitter winter night some years ago. "I didn't know ghosts got cold," I said aloud, waking from a deep sleep, as I moved over in bed to make room for her.

On a fall morning in 1987, Barbara Beebe checks two hives to see if the bees have stored enough honey for their survival in the coming winter. Susan Beebe, her daughter, takes notes.   *Palladium print by Jed Devine*

Kitchen of Lettie's House in summer 2006.   *Photo by Linda S. DeRosa*

3 *Oliver Morse House — "The Old House"* By Carleton W. Morse and Michael J. Trigilio

Note: The first part of the following text is taken from a paper written by Carleton Warren Morse in 1974 titled "Island Heritage." Since Carleton Morse wrote this island history, the eighth, ninth, tenth and eleventh generations have also enjoyed life on Morse Island.

Of the hundreds of islands, large and small, fringing the 3000-mile Maine coastline from Kittery to Lubec, probably few are still called home by direct descendents of their original pioneer settlers. The first known settlers on Morse Island (so called as early as 1760) were John and Lydia (Bradford) Morse, his wife. They established a farm home, building a small log house and a barn at the top of the hill some two hundred yards south of the landing at the northeast point. No trace of this first house remains today, but the old well, filled with stones in later years to exclude children and sheep, remains to indicate the approximate homesite. It is said that when John Morse started to dig his well, he uncovered an Indian grave, re-interred the remains, and dug his well in another spot. This story is very likely true, as the field and beach area just east of the first house site, having an abundant supply of good spring water, was once the site of an Indian summer village.

Simeon, a brother of John Morse, married Prudence Bradford, a sister of Lydia, both of the Bradford women being great-great-granddaughters of William Bradford of Plymouth, Massachusetts. Simeon and one of the Bradford men were both lost at sea from their fishing vessel near Isle au Haut.

Three sons of John Morse, Oliver, Cornelius, and Edward, were next

Oliver Morse house in the summer of 2006.   *Photo by Mike Trigilio*

Oliver Morse homestead on Morse's Island circa 1840s.   *Photo courtesy of Mike Trigilio*

to occupy the island homestead. Oliver, grandfather of the writer, was born in 1813 and died on February 20, 1888. He was a shipbuilder, house carpenter, farmer and fisherman, and he built the next two farm homes, the first being his own house, still standing straight and square and now the home of the writer, [Carlton W. Morse]. It was built about 1835, and construction included a large barn to house twelve to fifteen head of cattle and some thirty tons of hay. A stone foundation and stone barnyard walls are all that remain of the old barn, which blew down in 1910. Oliver also carved a sundial on a windowsill in the Old House, which can still be used today. The second floor of the house was used to dry corn for the many animals that lived in the barn. Oliver was also a selectman in town and at one time paid his road taxes by building a road to the lower end of the island and maintaining it. Oliver married his wife, Mary, in 1839 (about four years after the Old House was built).

At about this time Oliver and Cornelius worked together to construct the present large stone wharf. Visitors never cease to comment on and wonder how some of the great stones in the wharf, especially on its northeast and most storm-exposed area, were floated in and accurately positioned. This wharf is fifty-eight feet in width and of equal length with maximum height of about twelve feet. A large fish salting and drying establishment, thirty-eight feet wide by forty feet long with three floors, was built on the wharf. Two ten-foot wide doors permitted entry to the large storage shed or to the wharf with ox carts. One end of the shed extended over the ledges to tide water at the westerly side of the main building.

Three Morse brothers, Oliver, Cornelius, and Edward, engaged in shipbuilding and built a number of fishing schooners on the island and others at the shipyard once located at the head of Friendship Harbor.

Three schooners, the *Planter, Eastern Star*, and the *Edward Morse* were built at and owned and operated from Morse Island.

Warren Morse, one of the three sons of Oliver and Mary (McFarland) Morse, was born on the island on October 23, 1841. A second son, Albert, was lost at sea, and Charles, the younger brother, died at Lubec from sickness contracted while on a fishing voyage.

Warren, at a very early age, was interested in the boat-building trade and worked in his father's shop on the third floor of the fish house on Morse Island's wharf. He went on numerous fishing voyages with his father from the island and on a number of fishing vessels out of Gloucester, returning to his island home in Friendship in 1869 because of illness to his father, Oliver. The following year, 1870, Warren started boat building in the former salt fish house on the wharf. Here he built small craft of many sizes and types, including the first of the deep draft Friendship sloops up to 45 feet in length. The small craft included a fleet of sailing dories for Camp Durrell on Crotch Island in Friendship, a larger mahogany sailing dory for the daughter of Harriet Beecher Stowe, and a number of yachts. In addition he built many working sloops, then most in demand for the lobster and trawl fishing trade. The house had a schoolroom from 1891 to 1903. The town paid Warren for the use of the schoolroom. Warren served as a Friendship selectmen in 1874. He married his wife, Evelyn, in 1874; he died in November 1905.[1]

"The Old House," as it is now called, was passed down to Carleton Warren Morse (1897-1986), son of Warren. Carleton and his wife, Hazel, had two daughters, Virginia Morse Ward and Barbara Morse Townsend. Carleton's deep love for the Old House and Morse Island is shown to the current day. Carleton began to care and update the house for future generations. A dirt floor in the house became a kitchen, the fields and gardens were tended to, and water was brought into the house. The first flush toilet was installed in the 1970s; about the same time, Carleton added electricity. In 1973 a tractor shed was built. His labor can be found in woodcarvings, tools, and intricate details found throughout the Old House.

Barbara Morse Townsend and her husband, Jim, along with their daughters, Bonnie and Betsey, continued Carleton's love and care for the house throughout their lives by continuing to renew the Old House inside and out with a new roof, new shingles, and solar power.

The Old House has now passed onto Michael James Trigilio, grandson of Barbara (Morse) and Jim Townsend and son of Betsey Townsend Trigilio. In recent years, Michael has been instrumental in rebuilding the barn of years' past. In July 2005 an old-fashioned barn raising took place on the site of the original barn. Gary Baird, son-in-law of Virginia Morse Ward, designed the barn, thus keeping the entire project in the Morse family. Michael now frequents the Old House with his wife and three children, along with many Morse relatives who visit or live on the island.

Crotch Island rowing dories designed and built by Warren Morse.

Photo courtesy of Friendship Museum

Reprint of original photo (1874) showing first yacht built by Warren and Oliver Morse to "Pilot Boat" model and the owners specifications. The building, taken down in 1962, was built by Oliver Morse about 1830 as a fish salting and drying business, which also provided salt, trawling gear and new dories for a sizeable fleet of schooners and sloops then engaged in supplying the two fish salting establishments on Morses Island. The second fish house was owned by Cornelius Morse and is shown in the background of photo but with its main building obscured by trees. Bowsprit of Cornelius Morses fishing schooner show above fish shed roof and in distant background is the John Morse home and barn on Friendship Long Island with house and connecting barn originally built by James Murphy also showing on what was long known as Murphy's Point

Carleton Warren Morse
October 1974

The first yacht, a "pilot boat," built by Warren and Oliver Morse

Photo courtesy of Robert S. Lash, Jr.

Personal note by Carleton Warren Morse.   *Courtesy of Robert S. Lash, Jr.*

II Floating Homes

Well, Well, Well

Those of you who were here in the summer of 1965 may recall what a dry year it was. Wells went dry that year that had never been known to dry up before. Friendship was in dire straits for water. Visiting boats were refused water, cars and lawns were unwashed and unwatered, and many a spigot around town was dry for weeks.

This is a difficult situation and calls for drastic measures. Groups of local citizens put their heads together in consulation, and the town fathers met with committees to try to alleviate the situation, all to no avail.

Finally a solution to this dilemma became apparent during a discussion being carried on by a group of fishermen. One of the men remembered there was a deep well on Friendship Long Island that had long ago been abandoned but which still held an abundance of some of the finest water in the state.

Now the only problem was how to get that beautiful crystal clear water to the mainland where it would do some good. It was too far to pipe it and too costly to haul it by the barrelful, so the problem seemed no nearer solved than before.

However, there is always on ingenious fellow in every crowd. This time it was Stan Simmons, who recalled his father had moved a whole well to the mainland from Bremen Long Island. Stan recounted how it had been quite an undertaking, but everything had gone smoothly until Stan's father was approaching the wharf on the mainland. One of the big timbers supporting most of the weight of the well cracked under the strain, a couple of lines snapped, and just as the boat was being docked, the whole kit and caboodle slipped overboard. Luckily it was high water, and so when the tide went out, the well was easily retrieved and hauled to high ground, but Stan says to this day that well water tastes salty at high tide.

Taken from *The Friendship Sloop Race Book*, July 1967, page 15

By Marguerite C. Sylvester

Our ancestors were very adept at moving all sorts of objects such as a blacksmith shop, a school, and even houses. If you don't like where your shed, shop, school, or house is located, MOVE IT. It was a common occurrence in "the old days." The Wolfgrover blacksmith shop was moved across the street and became a schoolhouse. A small structure on Jameson Point was floated over to Bradford Point at high tide and is now called Bertha Young's "little house." The wooden schoolhouse was stealthily moved in the dark of night by rugged men and a team of oxen to a more desirable location for some families. To stop this practice, a brick schoolhouse was erected in 1850. It has remained put ever since.[1]

The crowning move was to relocate a house from an island to the mainland. Often the first settlers located on the islands just off the coast. As more pioneers arrived, there was safety in numbers, and many families literally moved their homes to the mainland. With the advent of engine-powered fishing boats in the 1920s, it was no longer necessary for Muscongus Bay fishermen to live on the islands. Often whole communities began to move to the mainland.

Here are three examples of this type of move. The "Chub" Patch house floated from Cranberry Island to Friendship Harbor; the Melvin Simmons house sailed on smooth waters from Bremen Long Island to Hatchet Cove, and Elizabeth Porcher's home, previously Melvin Simmons's store on Bremen Long Island, followed the Simmons homestead shortly thereafter. Let's examine these stories.

Hatchet Cove

"Black angel of the waterfront"

Photo by Polly Jones

Three shags glide by, their golden pouches saluting the sun.
One swoops off,
The other two, mother and adolescent child
Chase fish in our cove.
A yellowlegs darts between them
Then dances by fishing on the rim of the sea water.
Puffy white clouds float overhead;
The shags float too, heads underwater
Backs sticking up.
One catches and gulps down a pink crab.
Then they swim off, backed by a rock covered
With brown gold-tipped seaweed.
The yellowlegs darts swiftly around the water's edge
Catching small fish, his head bobbing up and down.
Drying out and resting on a bed of mussel shells,
The shags spread out their wings,
Black angel of the waterfront.

Cicily Aikman Scherer

5 *Melvin Simmons House— From the Island to the Mainland* By Lynn Meyer

Halfway down Hatchet Cove, on the inland side, stands a little green house on a granite ledge. The sign reads: *The Ledges-Mid Reed.* This is the home of Friendship's oldest resident and recipient of the Boston Post Cane for Friendship, ninety-nine-year old Mid Reed. The house was built for her in the nineteen thirties by her husband, Bud Reed. Her story holds the key to several of the surrounding houses as well.

Mid was once Mildred Simmons of Bremen Long Island, where her father, Melvin Simmons, owned and ran the general store. Her mother, Lottie (McLain) Simmons, came from a line of fishermen/boat builders credited with the early development of Muscongus Bay fishing vessels. Mid is descended from Carters, Priors, Morses, and McLains, a mixture best described as the Bremen Long Island clan and responsible for this area's notable reputation in boat building culminating in the celebrated Friendship sloop. (So named when Wilbur Morse left Bremen Long Island for Friendship and the beautiful, seaworthy boats came to national attention there.) Mid's great-grandmother was Wilbur Morse's sister Mary. Her grandfather, Eugene McLain, was a prominent boat builder of his generation, who was tragically drowned in 1911, when thrown from the bow of the *Martha E*, a 45-foot schooner which he built himself. Mid's grandmother, Martha (Carter) McLain, sewed sails for her husband's sloops on a treadle sewing machine.

The Simmons family homestead sat on the barren shore of Bremen Long Island, several hundred yards from the store. The house had been built by John Day and Eugene's brother Robert McLain in 1905; the store a year or so later.

Melvin Simmons, according to his grandson, was one of the first in the area to put an engine into his Friendship sloop. The arrival of motorized fishing changed the dynamics of island life, making it not so necessary to live close to the fishing areas. People began leaving the islands for the conveniences and opportunities of mainland living. After the entrepreneurial Wilbur Morse left, Bremen Long Island suffered an economic decline, and in 1927 (just prior to the national depression) Mid's father decided to close the Bremen Long Island store and move house and store to Friendship. Melvin Simmons is remembered as a kind-hearted, generous man. "There is nothing he wouldn't do for you," his family said. Few people realized that as the store drifted off to Friendship, any unpaid accounts of his island neighbors drifted away with it.

Twenty-year-old Mid remembered the move just as clearly nearly eighty years later, describing it fondly as " a beautiful day."[1] Her younger sister Glenys, however, recalls not wanting to leave the island and hiding in some bushes till she was finally found and brought along.

On moving day, December 13, 1927, a Boothbay man came with his nephew (Bud Reed) and his friend (Danny Davis) and loaded the homestead up on an old skow.[2] The skow was pushed along by boats that were joined in by other boats that came up to see what was going on and stopped to lend a hand.

The family floated peacefully along between Bremen Long Island and Cow Island, while Lottie got a big meal together. The ride was so smooth that not a dish was cracked nor a piece of furniture out of place.

Papa, Mama, Ralph, Myrtle and Mid at the house on Bremen Long Island.

Photo courtesy of Mid Reed

Her legendary biscuits rose to perfection that day (although rumor has it that a previous batch burned, were tossed overboard, and last seen with their little black bottoms pitching and bobbing off to Monhegan). Forty-five minutes after leaving Bremen Long Island, the family and house came around Martin Point and ashore at Hatchet Cove, Friendship.

Mid confesses to not knowing the logistics about securing the building, because she was more interested in meeting up with her sister Myrtle, who had already married and moved ahead to Friendship. The building spent the night on the waterside and the next day was pulled up by draft horses to a place along Martin Point Road where a hole had been dug and foundation laid for it.

How does one top off an already unforgettable move? Well, Edna married Danny Davis and moved to Waldoboro, while Mid married Bud Reed, who built for her the little house across the street.

Lottie and Mellie (with Grammy McLain) raised their family and continued to live in the homestead the rest of their lives. It passed on to their youngest son, Melvin, who sold it to Dave and Penny Reckards when he later moved to Cushing.

Glenys, sister to Mildred, married Mertland Harrington, settling on property they bought to the north side and adjoining the family homestead. She still lives there with her son, Bruce Winslow, just a short distance from Mid.

Mid continues to live in the little green house with her grandson, still doing her daily chores and cooking. She will be one hundred years old on Halloween 2007. To what does she attribute her longevity? "They made 'em good in the old days," said Mid. But credit also goes to God, who "got all the pieces hooked up right," she said.

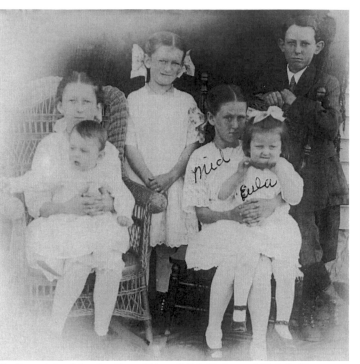

Left to right: Myrtle, Stan, Edna, Mid, Eula, and Ralph Simmons.
Photo from the collection of the Reed Family

The stove on which biscuits were baked as it looks in the Reckards's home today. *Photo by Carol Hoch*

The Melvin Simmons house from the water, in summer 2006.

Photo by Elaine Lang Cornett

Glenys Harrington's house.

Photo by Carol Hoch

Mid Reed – *One proud woman!*

Photo by Linda S. DeRosa

Mid Reed's house.

Photo by Carol Hoch

The Melvin Simmons house in Summer 2006.

Photo by Elaine Lang Cornett

6 *Melvin Simmons Store* By David Edwards

The Melvin Simmons family lived in a home built in 1905 by John Day and Robert McClain on Bremen Long Island. About a year later he built a general store and wharf on the shore, which became known as "Simmons landing." Goods were sometimes delivered to the store by coastal freighter and sometimes brought to Bremen Long Island by Melvin himself in his sloop *Stanley L.*[1] Times were different then, and men gathered around the potbellied stove to talk of boat designs. By 1928, Melvin Simmons, fisherman and storekeeper, who had already relocated his home to Hatchet Cove in Friendship in 1927, decided to repeat the process with his store. He loaded his store on a barge and towed it with his large fishing boat through the Cow Island Gut, across the Medomak River, around Martin Point and into Hatchet Cove, a process that took several days. The store was hauled up over the ledges to its present site on Martin Point Road by draft horses turning large windlasses.

Melvin Simmons store on Bremen Long Island. The Melvin Simmons house is at left.

Photo courtesy Bremen Historical Society

Mel Simmons sold his store to his brother, Emerson, who converted it, with minor additions, into a dwelling for himself and his wife, Ada Collamore. Ada inherited the property on Emerson's death, and at the time of her death, passed it on to her second husband, fisherman and boat builder Jim Murphy.

In 1947 Jim moved out of his house for the summer and rented it to Dr. Herbert Randolph Edwards of New York City. The Edwards family returned as renters not only the following year but off and on for subse-

The front of the Melvin Simmons store in 2006.
Photo by Fran Richardson

quent summers until 1960. That year Elizabeth Porcher, Mrs. Edwards' sister, purchased the house, a small camp on the shore, and four acres of land from Jim Murphy and became a year-round resident of Friendship.

Jim continued to operate the boat shop for two more years and in 1962 deeded the remaining land to Mrs. Porcher. A crew of trustees from the Thomaston Prison Farm came to take down the boat shop, leaving the site undeveloped until much later.

After Mrs. Porcher's death in 1993, her sister, Carol Kemerer Edwards, took up residence in the former store where her children,

Carol Edwards at her 100th birthday party in 2001. *Photo by Elizabeth K. Bunbury*

grandchildren, and great-grandchildren enjoyed their summer vacations. Moving back into her home in Connecticut, Mrs. Edwards continued to return for summer visits, highlighted by her 100th birthday party in the Hahn Community Center in 2001.

In 2003 her sons David and Kem Edwards divided the land into separate parcels with Kem and his wife, Phoebe, retaining the old family place and David and his wife, Barbara, building their new cottage nearer the ocean's edge in June 2004. David and Barbara reside in Connecticut during the winter but spend the remaining three seasons of the year nestled on the shores of Hatchet Cove.

Living room in 2006.
Photo by Fran Richardson

The east side of the Melvin Simmons store in 1964.
Pen-and-ink drawing by Sam Cady

7 *Chub Patch House* By Priscilla Wilder Ambrose

The harbor area at Cranberry Island in Minister's Gut was one of the local thriving fishing communities existing in the 19th century, complete with a schoolhouse and many fine homes even before life on the mainland in Friendship became established. The settlers in the early 19th century lived on the islands. This was to provide safety from the Indians and to be closer to the fishing banks which were their main reason for emigrating here from Europe via Massachusetts even before 1800.[1]

The islands in Muscongus Bay – Friendship Long, Cranberry, Bremen Long, Hungry, Morse, and Monhegan, to name many– were inhabited by these settlers until the Indian threat waned and the gasoline engine provided more dependable travel to the fishing banks. The automobile was becoming established with ever-improving roads to accommodate it, decreasing the use of waterways as the major highways.

It's astonishing to think that folks who had lived on the islands for a century eventually realized the mainland might be a more practical place to live. Many moved in. Some even thought it might make good sense to bring their island home with them – well built, attractive on the whole, and, after all, home. One would think there would have been quite a business in house-moving to the mainland. It was possible but complicated. Besides all the other challenges,

a body of water had to be navigated. Several houses are known to have been brought over from the islands, but so far a photograph of the actual moving event has yet to be discovered.

A handsome house on Davis Point, now called the Chub Patch House, is one such house that came from Cranberry Island. It was built there in 1848 and at the time of its crossing in 1910 was owned by the

Location of the Chub Patch house on Cranberry Island.

Photo courtesy Friendship Museum

The north and west sides of Chub Patch house in Summer 2006.

Photo by Polly Jones

Elbridge Burns family. Captain Bob Lash tells of the incident in a taped discussion with Bill Jameson in 1967 referring to the house on the island:

    Bill: 'Now who had that?'
    Bob: 'Bridge Burns had it. Leslie's father up here. And I was with him the time they moved it off with a vessel.'
    Bill: 'What did they use to move it off with?'
    Bob: 'Well, this Giles from Boothbay had a big scow and took this lobster smack schooner and towed it off. Landed on Ev's shore there (Everin Davis).'[2]

Betty Roberts, long-time secretary of the Friendship Sloop Society, has written about some dramatic incidents that occurred during the crossing. According to stories told her by the old-timers, even the chimney was moved intact. And the lady of the house, Phoebe Burns, realizing it was time for supper as the structure was floating across the bay, stood right up to the stove and prepared the meal. Alas, one mishap did take place when the well fell overboard into the harbor. They were able to retrieve it, but local lore says they were never able to get all the salt out of it again.[3]

The Burnses must have been delighted when their island home was successfully situated on a bank overlooking the harbor up above the bustling Jameson and Wotton Wharf. Years later, in 1926, the Patch family from Massachusetts purchased the house, moved in, and eventually lived there on a year-round basis. During their time in residence, they built a two-story ell and another upstairs bedroom while incorporating the front porch into the interior. It remains a handsome landmark today, while we will always delight in its seagoin' history.

The east side of Chub Patch house, facing Friendship Harbor in Summer 2006.

Photo by Polly Jones

III The Village

The Benner Boats

Since 1994, Arnold and Wayne Benner's lighted boats have been a Christmas greeting to all. Arnold's daughter, Becky, was a graduate student in Iowa and missed the July launching of the *Becky Jean II*, named for her. Arnold strung the boat with lights to surprise both Becky and her brother Derek when they came to Friendship for their Christmas breaks. Wayne also decorated his boat, the *Megan Jill*, and the tradition was born. Arnold and Wayne have lighted the boats for the holiday each year since then. Christmas 1999, the *Becky Jean II* was at the Lash Boat Yard for a new engine. To keep the tradition, a lighted tree was placed on the bow, and Wesley Lash powered the lights.

Photo by Robert Cornett

8 *The Corner* By Patricia Winchenbach

Every town has its "happening" place, the hub of activity, that part of town where folks can get their errands done and probably bump into a few friends and neighbors along the way. If you're a fairly new resident or vacationer in Friendship, you might refer to that part of town as the village, or the center of town, but, if you *grew up* here, you probably know that in this little town if you wanted to buy milk, mail a card, hear the latest gossip, or run into your neighbor, you had to "go up the corner."

The Corner actually refers to the stretch of town that starts at the Advent Church and extends down to the Post Office. In that immediate vicinity, you can go to church (Methodist or Advent), pay your taxes and check out the museum display at the town office; say "Howdy" to your neighbor on your left; check out a book at the library; buy a can of paint or a part for your furnace at the hardware store; purchase an antique for someone special or some sparkling earrings for your girlfriend (or boyfriend) at the antique/gift store; say "Howdy," to your neighbor on your right; buy a gallon of milk, a bunch of bananas, and a hot cup of coffee, gas up your car, and say "Howdy," to your brother-in-law while you're there at Wallace's Market. Then, you can drop on down to the US Post Office, mail your letters, and say "Howdy" to the folks in there; circle back around School Square on the back side of The Corner, pick up your kids at school and let them play at the playground for a bit while you stop into the B&B and make a reservation for Aunt Sally for when she

Wink's Market at The Corner.

Photo courtesy of Penobscot Marine Museum

comes for two weeks this summer, sign her up for kayaking lessons, and say "Howdy" to the folks walking by as you leave.

If you ask any "old" folks in town why they call it The Corner, they'll tell you that it's called that because, well, that's what it is! It's the corner where one has to turn either left or right— where one runs out of Route 220 and must turn left on Rte. 97 to head north out of town, or right to go down to the harbor. That's not to say though that it's *just* a corner. In the same breath, these old-timers will tell you that that was where Lil and Al Pottle's store sat, and they'll quickly go on to tell you about all the local businesses that drew the townspeople, both young and old, to that part of town. The buildings have changed somewhat; some have burned down, and others have been raised up.

Lil and Al Pottle were not the original owners of the two-story building that sat directly at the right hand side of the corner. In the early 1900s it held Ida Francis's millinery shop— apparently Ms. Francis made some mighty fine hats in her day— while upstairs was Lizzie Stone's dressmaking shop.[1] However, when Al and Lil bought it, they operated a candy store downstairs, using the upstairs as their residence. Many people today remember that the store had a wonderful front porch, which was a favorite summertime gathering place for gents from the town who'd sit for hours, spilling the town gossip and keeping an eye on the town's activity; in the wintertime, they moved inside around the old potbelly stove, making use of spitoons that were in place for the tobacco chewers. Of course, there was a steady flow of children too, who came to make the sweetest and best trade for their pennies. When the building changed hands again, the downstairs became a restaurant opened by Nelson and Marie Lash with the help of their daughter, Joan, serving home-cooked meals such as fish chowder and baked beans. The building was eventually moved and now sits on Cottage Street.

At the top of the hill where the library is now, a huge two-story building named Westerland Hall (later known as Ray's Hall) once stood. The front of the building was a general store and the large hall was used for dances, graduations, rummage sales, and other such large-scale to-dos.[2] Later the front part of the building would become a drugstore with a popular soda fountain where sweethearts and "sweet-tooths" would linger. When Wallace & Winchenpaw bought the building around 1925, they ran a grocery store in the front, and continued to use the hall for large events. A stage facilitated live plays performed by touring troupes and local theatre guilds. Some locals even remember roller-skating and playing basketball at the hall, but most memorable to many of the local mature folks are the movies that were shown there— silent and in black and white. One of the town's former residents, Eleanor "Mamie" Winchenbach, kept an ongoing diary during the years when she was a

teenager. Most days she wrote something like: "Corner at nite. [sic]. Not many around." (5/2/1932) or "Had fun at the corner. Big crowd around." (4/7/1933). Her diary often records the movies that played there as well. Her February 6, 1932 entry says, "Movies at night. 'Ladies Love Brutes.' Good, awful sad," and on May 1, 1935, she wrote: "Movies at corner…. 'Peck's Bad Boy' (Jackie Searl & Jackie Cooper) Good."[3]

Just down the road a block or two, Les Thompson's Store (now Wallace's market) carried groceries and kerosene, while upstairs his wife sold dry goods such as cloth, as well as silverware, toys, and jewelry. Next door to that, Eda Lawry was running a beauty parlor. Up the road on the other side of Ray's Hall another store, Sid Prior's store, offered haircuts and candy, then expanded to carry hardware, paint, rope, and other such goods; that building still stands today and is still our local source of hardware and other needs.

The town at one time had three grocery stores, and of course Dr. Hahn kept office hours in his home on the left side of The Corner not so many years ago. Over the years, that strip known as The Corner has also included Friendship's high school (formerly located across the street from the Advent Church)[4], a barbershop, the local coffin shop, the village blacksmith shop (another fun place to linger and watch), and many other businesses that have come and gone. Clearly though, after all these years, whatever you call it— the village, uptown, downtown or The Corner— it's still the place to get your chores done, a place to go to school, a place to work or play, a place to worship, and a real fine place to run into your neighbor.

The Corner.

Photo courtesy of Jameson family collection

9 *Zenas Cook II House* *By Eleanor Cook Lang*

On the top of Cook's Hill in the very center of Friendship stands a large, handsome Federal style house now known as the Outsider's Inn — a B&B run by Bill and Debbie Michaud. Built about 1834-35 by Zenas Cook, son of Elijah and grandnephew of his namesake — original settler Zenas Cook — it has a long history as a center of Friendship life. The "ell" section, which was a general store for many years, had a second story added in 1860. Zenas Cook II was a man of many talents.

Besides the general store, he had a partnership in the shipbuilding firm of Cook & Morse in Waldoboro. He was a Justice of the Peace and held various other town offices through the years. He was instrumental in having the present Methodist Church built in 1840.

Zenas married Mary Bradford, daughter of Fredrick Bradford I, in 1837. Melville Bradford Cook, Civil War hero, ship captain, author, and businessman, was their son. In September 1861 Melville was the first man from Friendship to enlist in the Thomaston Company of the 1st Maine Cavalry, Company B, commanded by General J. P. Cilley. He

Photo by Elaine Lang Cornett

was wounded three times, one time seriously, and served until the end of the war. In the year of 1865 he held the rank of first sergeant and was mustered out at Petersburg.[1] Melville (or "Mel"), as did his father, had the interests of Friendship very much at heart and is responsible for editing and transcribing some of the old town records which otherwise would be lost today. He married Anna C. Albee, a graduate of the New England Conservatory of Music.[2] They had one daughter, Grace, who married Dr. Edward Abbott of Bridgton, Maine. Mr. Cook served as Knox County Commissioner from 1893 to 1898 and County Treasurer 1899-1900. About 1900, Mel moved to Bridgton to live with his daughter.

Melville Cook, First Sergeant, the first man from Friendship to enlist in 1st Maine Cavalry.   *Photo courtesy of the Jameson family collection*

Zenas and Mary Cook also had a daughter, Ida, who married Captain Fernando Francis. In 1886, while on a trip with their little son in a schooner named for Ida, the family experienced a terrible storm that left the ship disabled and only half afloat. They survived for nearly a month on salt-water-soaked hardtack and such other supplies as they could fish out of the hold. They cooked what they could over a kerosene lamp, including their pet parrot, for which they had no food anyway. A Captain Bjocquist, sailing his Russian bark, *Bacchus* to London, England, finally rescued them. After surviving the ordeal, Ida wrote a letter to Ella Davis Cook dated March 24, 1886. This excerpt describes in a few words how dire their circumstances were: "Little Mellie was put in a bag and hung up high to keep him dry and warm. He had to be guarded both day and night because the sailors were so hungry, they would have eaten him."[3] My father, Raymond Cook, who was twelve years old at the time, remembered very well how the church bells were rung when the news arrived in Friendship that Captain Francis and his family were safe in London. Ida Francis vowed never to go to sea again, but her husband captained several more ships before his retirement.

I have not been able to establish whether either Mel or Ida ever owned or lived in Zenas Cook's house after they were grown and married, but I do know that ownership of the house passed into the hands of Dr. William Hahn about 1900, around the time that Zenas Cook died. Dr. Hahn was another man to whom Friendship owes a great deal. He practiced in Friendship for over fifty years, helping several generations of citizens into the world as well as out of it. Rich and poor alike received equal attention. He was especially fond of children, and his waiting room contained several things of interest to them. One favorite was a pool table. In the main room on the first floor, the beautiful pressed tin ceiling still has the base part of the light fixtures that hung over the table, which they were allowed to come in and use any time his office was open. That way he successfully cultivated their friendship

Original light fixture and tin ceiling.

Photo by Elaine Lang Cornett

A section of the livingroom and fireplace.

Photo by Elaine Lang Cornett

Livingroom of the Zenas Cook II house in 1930s.   *photo courtesy Morton family collection*

and trust. Among other interesting things the Michauds have found and preserved in his memory is a 1915 Maine number plate from Dr. Hahn's first car (before that, it was horse and buggy!). I am also told that he covered the islands by boat and on foot, as long as he was able. He was very interested the history of Friendship and its founding families and kept extensive records of his research, which can be found now in the Friendship Public Library.

Dr. Hahn died in 1952, leaving the house and other property to his wife, Florence. They had no children of their own, but saw the children of Friendship as part of their family. The Hahn Community Center was given to the town by Mrs. Hahn in honor of her husband. She left the house to relatives, who sold it to Paul and Kay Burgess, who used it as a summer house. It then passed into other hands and was a rental property for a while. In 1986 Bill and Debbie Michaud bought the house, renovated it, and opened it as a bed-and-breakfast in 1987. They continue the tradition of this beautiful old house by being important members of the community. Bill, among other things, runs a rental and guide service for visiting kayakers and is well known as an auctioneer at local charity events.

The Zenas Cook II house in 2006.

Photo by Elaine Lang Cornett

10 *Captain William Jameson Farm— Site of the Earliest Frame House* By Celia Lash Briggs

The Jameson name is deeply woven into the history of Meduncook Plantation. One can find it among a list of the earliest settlers' names in the 1740s and there are still Jamesons living in Friendship. Paul Jameson, who came to the eastward with his brothers Samuel and Alexander, settled here and raised ten children.[1] He purchased property from Asa Thomas for "consideration of one barley corn"[2] and together Paul and Asa built the first frame house in the settlement on a rise of land above Blackfish Cove. All earlier homes in the plantation had been constructed of logs. Asa had no family of his own and lived with the Jamesons until his death. What happened to this house is not known, but the remains of the cellar could still be found in the early 1900s in the field near the present house on Shipyard Lane.[3]

This red cape and barn were built in 1805 by Paul's son William. He was a sea captain who was the commander of a number of vessels, including the brig *Venus* that he sailed to the West Indies. He built his home well, as the house has lasted over two hundred years and is still held together by the original wooden pegs. The half timbers supporting the main story were later sistered with sawn joists, but the house still rests on the granite blocks it was built on. The kitchen wainscot, which is still there, was made from one single wide board. Old wide pine plank floors continue to add charm throughout the rooms.

The house was passed onto his son, another Captain William Jameson. As a boy he received his education at the log schoolhouse near Goose River. He later told stories of wolves and bear that he saw on his long walks there and home again. When he was 12 he saved the town from a surprise attack by a British raiding party (see sidebar). At age 13 he witnessed the battle between the British brig *Boxer* and the American brig *Enterprise* off Monhegan Island. He "followed the seas for forty years" and "during his seafaring life he had been a castaway three times, and barely escaped death."[4]

William was married in 1828 to Mary Young, and together they had

Photo by Victor Motyka

seven children, six of whom survived to adulthood. Mary passed away when the youngest was only five years old. He married Mary Johnston the following year, and together they had a son. For a short time, beginning in 1845, Captain Jameson became the keeper at the Franklin Island lighthouse.

Captain William Jameson
Photo courtesy of Jameson family collection

The homestead was a working farm with ample gardens and pasture for cows, sheep, and a horse.[5] The barn that now stands in the dooryard may be a replacement of an earlier one, for construction techniques suggest a date later than 1805. For many years, there had been no other homes near the farm, but in the mid-1800s the village grew and the farm was no longer as isolated.

William died in 1890, and his second wife died in 1895. His oldest daughter, Elmira, was crippled and never married. She remained in the house until her death in 1897. Winthrop and Lavinia Whitney (daughter of William's son Francis) had moved in to care for Elmira, and they were the next owners of the house. At a later date the farm's ownership was transferred to people outside the Jameson family. The farm had been an integral part of the Jameson family for over one hundred and fifty years.

Russell Neal, owner of the farm in the 1950s and 1960s. *Photo courtesy of Arlene Neal*

Lives of Service

Paul Jameson was the Captain of the Meduncook Company during the Revolutionary War. He and his son William were taken prisoner by British soldiers, but they escaped. When Paul was an old man he raised his cane, and threatened to strike Tory Benjamin Bradford who had betrayed him. This patriotism proved to be a strong family trait. Captain Robert Jameson and his crew of two from Meduncook were participants in the Boston Tea Party. They had just arrived in Boston with a load of cordwood when Lord North's tea ships were lying at anchor in the harbor. They disguised themselves as Indians and helped dispose of the tea into Boston Harbor.[1]

During the War of 1812, Paul's grandson, William Jr., at the age of 13, rode through town Paul Revere style to warn folk that the British were sneaking into the harbor to steal the fishing fleet. After spreading the alarm, he took up his flintlock and headed to Bradford's Point to join with other men who were guarding the settlement. On his way he heard the voices of British soldiers who were rowing up the Meduncook River, and he fired on them, scaring them into retreat. The soldiers returned to their man-of-war, which was anchored off of Eastern Egg Rock.

During the Civil War, when his three sons, Francis Gracia, Jonah, and Lafayette, enlisted with the 21st Regiment, retired Captain William Jameson Jr. was willing to serve also and is said to have stated, "and the old man too, if they want him." On July 25, 1863 the youngest son, Lafayette, died near Port Hudson, Louisiana from dysentery, a disease that claimed many soldiers.[2] His brother Jonah was struck by a Confederate bullet, but a buckle deflected the shot and spared his life.

In his later years, Capt. William Jameson Jr. also served a term as a state representative. Many brave acts from a family that Friendship is proud to lay claim to.

Jonah's vest showing a hole where a buckle deflected a bullet and spared his life during the Civil War. *Photo by Carol Hoch*

[1] William Hahn, *History of Friendship*, Friendship, ME, researched by William Hahn and compiled by Mary Carlson, section titled: "History of Friendship", p. 2.
[2] Courtney MacLachlan, *The Amanda Letters*, (Bowie, Maryland: Heritage Books, 2003) p.214.

11 *Nelson Thompson House— Man of Tenacity and Talent* By Marguerite C. Sylvester

Driving through Friendship, we often fail to recognize the tremendous heritage we have. Daily we pass beautiful historic homes; homes harboring stories of men and women of great strength of character; stories of ingenuity and courage; stories of devotion and determination; homes that left us a legacy that we can be proud of. One of these homes is the Nelson Thompson home.

Joseph Thompson, married to Lavina McClain of Cranberry Island, ran a general store on Cranberry Island. Nelson Thompson, one of their nine children born on Cranberry Island, started life as a fisherman. But that was not to be. Later he attended the Academy at Thomaston after which he taught several terms of school. But that, too, was not to be. [1]

In 1855 Nelson and his brother Robert followed their father's footsteps by building what is a Friendship landmark. You pass it nearly every day and hardly give it a second thought. You may even enter it to purchase your groceries, pay for gas, or just to get a cup of coffee. Recently, a model for the magazine, *Vogue Fall Extravaganza*, September 2006, [2] did a photo shoot at the store. (You can be sure that created quite a stir.) Many know it as "Archie's." Let's learn more about this familiar landmark and its creator, Nelson Thompson. It has a great story to tell.

The framework of the store, a one-story building, was hewn out by hand on Cranberry Island by Nelson's father, Joseph Thompson. Nelson and his brother Robert ran the store in partnership until Robert was lost on Cape Cod in the lobster smack *Delaware* which ran between Friendship and New York. [3]

Although Nelson and his brother Robert built a three story house on the mainland in 1864, Nelson had other talents. In a shipyard located on the shore in front of the Johnson house, Nelson built four schooners: the *Edward Morse* (30.2 tons), the *Clara Benner* (38.7 tons), the *Helen Thompson* (131.3 tons) and *The Three Sisters* (33.8) tons. [4]

Nelson was state representative between the years 1867 and 1869. In the 1878 state election, he was elected as senator for a one year term. His son, Les, was active within the community also; besides running the store, he was a postmaster and held the office of selectman.

When Nelson died in 1893, the house was left to Robert L. Thompson, known as "Les" Thompson, who had married Jessie Hamlin of Hyannis, Massachusetts. In his youth, before he became old enough to take over his father's business, he served on coastwise sailing vessels for a time. In 1887, before his father's death, Les hired Silas A. Morton to raise the roof adding another story and improving the appearance of the building. [5]

This enabled Les to sell small items in the room above the general store. Women and children were delighted with the offerings: a yard of calico, bed quilts, a jacket, curtains, flat irons, children's shoes, tiny dolls, small toys, and precious knickknacks. The store ledger indicated payment for bills often came in the form of services rendered such as labor on a schooner, $100.50. Often an amazing assortment of items of value such as cords of wood, white oak, mink skins, calf skins, hides, mackerel, pigs, eggs, butter, potatoes, tallow, and mittens were accepted as payment. [6] Not a recommended method of payment today.

Archie and Ivernia Wallace rented the small house across the street from the Thompsons for $6.00 a month from Alfred Morton. Archie, a lobster fisherman, later became constable for the town and was chosen in 1984 as the first Grand Marshall for the Friendship Day parade. [7] Ivernia worked in the clam factory and often worked for the "summer people." In 1942 they bought Les Thompson's properties but insisted that Les's family, now elderly, remain in the home.

Wallace's Market in summer 2006.

Photo by Linda S. DeRosa

Ivernia and Archie moved into the home where Ivernia became a housekeeper for Les and cared for Jessie's sister, Hattie Hamlin Dwyer, who was ill. As their little house on the corner had been extremely cold, Archie and Ivernia were glad the living room in Les's house had a metal grate in the floor over the furnace. The rising heat gave warmth to their bedroom on the second floor.

Although Ivernia was not fond of eels or 'coot', she would often make a tasty meal of fried eels for Les or would roast a 'coot', a game bird Les was fond of.

When Les died in January 1944, the store was taken over by Archie and Ivernia Wallace, who had often worked in the general store. Many of the people Ivernia worked for began trading there. The store became the center of Ivernia's life. Evenings it became a gathering place where fisherman could swap stories. The store remains a landmark not only locally, but as a familiar landmark to those near and afar. [8]

Ivernia's son, Bruce, gave a guided tour of the Nelson Thompson home with its wide floorboards, excellent woodwork, its many rooms— all restored to its original beauty. One gazes with awe at this 142-year-old home and feels a deep appreciation for the skills, strength, and capabilities of the men who built it.

Nelson Thompson house in summer 2006.

Photo by Elaine Lang Cornett

Friendship in Action

Walk in the woods hand in hand
with a child and discover lady slippers
And jack-in-the-pulpits.

Visit with one of Friendship's local
artists and admire their work.

Train a chick-a-dee to eat sunflower
seeds out of your hand.

Learn Maine lingo: harbah for harbor,
Rocklan' for Rockland, ayuh for yes.

Enjoy the full moon reflecting on
Friendship harbor or Hatchet Cove.

Breathe in the smell of Maine air on
clothes hung on the clothesline.

Marguerite C. Sylvester

Nelson Thompson house and barn/garage in fall 2006.

Photo by Linda S. DeRosa

12 *Webb Thompson House— Home of Master Seaman* By Marguerite C. Sylvester

Today we look at Friendship harbor and admire the many varieties of vessels: lobster boats, sloops, dories, catboats, and even an occasional cruise boat. What is missing? What about those great schooners of the past? We are proud of the skills of our seamen, young and old, but let us examine the life of a captain of one of those great ships that traveled from Friendship Harbor in the late 1800s to ports around the world: England, India, Japan.

N.Webb Thompson, son of Joseph and Lavina Thompson, who was born on Cranberry Island on January 23, 1846, is that captain. His schooling consisted of "a few weeks in a fishhouse" on his native island. For several years he pursued fishing as a means of support. Accumulating funds, he was able to purchase a lobster smack in which he carried lobsters to the Boston market. [1]

In 1870 Webb married Susie B. Morse, an accomplished and educated lady who had a successful career as a schoolteacher. Their home was built in 1875 by Webb's brother, Nelson Thompson.

Noting Webb's reliability, individuals in Boston assisted him in building a three-masted schooner, *M.E.Downer*, in 1872. In 1877, returning from England, his ship was in a collision with a brig in which the *Downer* was disabled and abandoned. The brig, however, survived but was found liable for the collision and was taken for damages.

The following year, Captain Thompson took temporary command of the bark *Bennington* of Boston and made a trip to England. Soon after his return, H.M. Bean of Camden built a three-masted schooner,

Webb Thompson house with wooden sidewalk.

From the collection of Marguerite C. Sylvester

John K. Souther by William P. Stubbs.

From a private collection

R. Bowers, for Captain Thompson. This was launched in 1880 and successfully commanded by him until 1889 when he was offered a position on a four-masted schooner, the *John K. Souther*, built in Thomaston by Washburn Bros. As captain of the *John K. Souther* he had an enviable reputation and made many a profitable trip for the owners and himself.

Tragedy came into the lives of the Thompsons when their daughter, Agnes M., born in 1875, died just two years after her birth. In 1890 their remaining child, Maurice E., only seventeen years old, died of typhoid fever. Their home became a place of sadness and discontent; accordingly, most of their time was spent at sea together.

Captain Thompson was an excellent example of a man who made his own opportunities and fortunes. He left us with a principle that he not only preached but practiced as well. "The only security for success in life is for a man to earn a dollar before he spends it." Good advice for us today.

Charlie Murphy lived in the Webb Thompson house in the 1900s. Charlie's grandfather, Emanuel Francis from Portugal, had stowed away on a ship coming to America in order to avoid being drafted into the Portuguese Navy. When he arrived here, no one could pronounce his name, so he assumed the name of Emanuel Francis.[2] His daughter Susan married Albion Murphy. Charlie, "Jack of all trades and master of many," was born in Friendship on Bradford Point in 1877. You name it, he's "been there and done that."[3]

Only nine years old, Charlie made enough money digging clams, 16 to18 bushels daily, to buy his school clothes. Hard to believe, but then clams were as low as 35 cents per bushel. As Charlie grew up, he ran the clam boat for the Burnham and Morrill "clam factory." Charlie recalls shucking clams, washing and salting them, then selling them for $3.75 a barrel to schooner handliners who used them as bait.[4]

Charles took great pride in the fact that he was one of the first lobster fishermen in the state to apply for a Maine lobster license in 1916. At the time of his retirement, he was the oldest lobsterman in the state

of Maine. At that time, Commissioner Greenleaf turned over the number one lobster license to Charles Murphy's great-grandson, Sherman Stanley of Monhegan Plantation, Maine. Thus it became LOBSTER CRAB CLASS III #1A.

Charles was the second man in Friendship harbor to get a gas-driven boat. Charlie explained, " When I first started lobstering, I used a sailboat or dory. We would get up at three a.m., fish out five or six miles off the coast and be back in at two-thirty or three p.m. so we could repair nets for the next day fishing."

He goes on, "Back then you could haul eighty to a hundred traps. There would be times you would get out to sea and the breezes stopped, and oh boy...it would take all your effort to get back to the mooring by late afternoon."[5]

When the *Cambridge*, in transit to Bangor from Boston with a cargo of food and seeds for spring planting in northern Maine, was wrecked on Old Man Ledge in 1886, Charlie's father, Albion Murphy, salvaged some of the bean seeds and rutabaga. They are a horticultural type bean that develop a string, so they're best if picked early. The rutabagas, with their high sugar content, were important as an alternative for hay for the oxen.

For years, Charlie planted beans and turnips in his

Charlie Murphy with firkin and geese.

From a private collection

Charlie Murphy at Stenger's wharf.

Photo courtesy of Tommy Stenger

garden. Charlie often used them as a stew bean. From that time on they became "Charlie Murphy Beans." Today because of their historical connection with an event that occurred over one hundred years ago, the legacy of the *Cambridge* lives on through these seeds in the Heirloom Seed Project under the direction of Neil Lash, teacher at Medomak Valley High School.[6]

Retiring after lobstering for seventy-five years, Charlie kept busy knitting nylon "heads" for lobster traps. Eldon E. Libby, interviewing Charlie for *The Shell News* in 1971, reported, "Charlie knits as he talks, his hands darting in and out of nylon cords as easily as an eel swimming downstream." With a grin, Charlie told the reporter, "I knit 2,500 heads last year and made about $200. Not many people today would work for $1.50 a day, would they?"[7]

Today, Kurt and Amy McCollett and their three sons live in the Webb Thompson house. Unaware of its historic value but in need of a larger home for their growing family, they purchased the home in Friendship. The lovely home still has many of its original special features: lovely beveled glass in the bay window and beautiful arches in the doorways. Amy revealed an interesting discovery in the kitchen; tucked away in a cupboard is the original flour barrel on a swivel that allows it to swing out with ease so one may conveniently reach the flour. An important part of the preparation for winter was to have a

barrel of flour on hand. Kurt pointed out a crate they were using as a woodbox with Webb Thompson's name and address handwritten on it.[8]

Only as the couple made cosmetic repairs did they realize their "diamond in the rough" had a relationship to the family's history. Amy's grandmother, Mary Lash Wotton, recently shared that in the early 1890s Amy's great-great-grandfather, John Lash, had been first mate on the *John K. Souther* under Captain Webb Thompson, the first owner of the house she was presently living in.[9]

Original tin ceiling in the Webb Thompson house.

Photo by Amy McCollett

Many years have passed, but once again the home is connected to Webb Thompson.

The Webb Thompson house in Fall 2006.

Photo by Elaine Lang Cornett

Original flour barrel still in use today.

Photo by Amy McCollett

A postal box addressed to N. (Webb) Thompson, presently used as a woodbox.

Photo by Amy McCollett

13 *Kitt Jameson House* By Marguerite C. Sylvester

One would hardly consider Friendship to be cosmopolitan. Yet if you look the word up in the dictionary, you will find the meaning: composed of elements gathered from various parts of the world. In this book, we learn that the Autio family had roots in Finland, the De la Noye (Delano) family crossed the Atlantic from Holland, Emanuel Francis came from Portugal, the Lawrys came from East Anglia, and the Jamesons had their origin in the Highland Clan of Gunn in northern Scotland. Certainly, Friendship is a cosmopolitan community.

"The Jamesons in America have all come from a common ancestry

Kitt Jameson house in fall 2006.

Photo by Elaine Lang Cornett

in Scotland. Some of their ancestral immigrants came to America direct-ly from their Scotland homes, while others first passed over into Ireland, where they found their way across the sea to this country." Jameson records indicate that Paul, born in Friendship, Maine in 1761, and William, born in 1764, were the descendants of William Jameson (1675), who came with a large company of immigrants known as Scots Irish from Northern Ireland.

William (1801), Friendship farmer and fisherman, a man more than six feet in height, followed the sea for forty years and for the greater part of this time was the master of a vessel. During his seafaring, he had been a castaway three times and barely escaped death. He filled many offices of public service in Friendship and was elected to the state legislature.[1]

Francis Gracia Jameson, grandson of William (1801), married to Ruby Ann Thompson, the daughter of Webb Thompson, owned the lovely home on the main street in Friendship. The children in the picture below are prob-ably Francis and Ruby's three daughters, Gertrude, Lavinia, and Kathryn, and their son, Sherman Tecumseh Jameson. Old deeds labeled "home place" among Kitt's papers show Joshua Thompson bought the place from William Jameson in December 1862 for thirty dollars. Francis G. Jameson, coastal sea captain, bought the property with a large apple orchard in the back yard from Joseph Thompson in 1868 for eleven hundred dollars.

William's three grandsons, Francis, Jonah, and Lafayette Jameson, served in the Civil War. Jonah served in the war for the Union in the 21st Maine Regiment under General Banks. In *Amanda's Letters* Lafayette wrote a letter from East New York indicating his homesick-ness, " I should like to be at home and gow [sic] at school this winter but it cannot be. wee have to go forth and fight the Battels of our Countary and put down this wicked Rebellion which is now rageing in the land."[2]

A copy of the Volunteer Discriptine Roll reveals that "Francis Gracia Jameson, mariner, was assigned to the 21st Maine regiment on 3/27/1862. Stationed at 'Camp Bank,' Baton Rouge, Louisiana. There, he was allot-ted $19.53 for clothing and $3.00 for a rubber blanket." Among the family mementos of the Civil War is a vest belonging to Jonah with a bullet hole and a note in the pocket stating the bullet was deflected off a buckle.[3]

Pat Jameson Havener shares another touching story about Francis Gracia Jameson, revealing his devotion to country and pride in his fellow service members. Francis, as long as he was able, would make wreaths of apple blossoms and take wheelbarrow loads of them to the cemetery and place flags and wreaths on the graves of Civil War veterans.

Family stories often reveal not only our strengths but also our idiosyn-crasies. Francis "had no love for a horse" (makes one wonder why). Rather than ride the stage to Waldoboro, he would walk. He would pass the stage

The Jameson family in front of their house circa 1875.

Apple blossoms still flourish at Kitt Jameson's house.

Photo by Margaret Wotton Gagnon

going uphill; they would pass him on the flat stretch. Hardy man of yesteryear walking those ten miles to Waldoboro.[4]

Francis Gracia Jameson's daughter, Kathryn, known to many as Kitt, lived in the home on Main Street. Kathryn attended Coburn Classical Institute in Waterville. Never married, she worked as bookkeeper for the Jameson and Wotton's store at the harbor.

Pat Jameson Havener has a treasured keepsake, a small suitcase belonging to her Aunt Kitt. One day she showed it to Pat and said, "This is yours, when I go." There was a complete set of toiletries necessary for travel: comb, brush, mirror, nail buffer, and boot hook.

Ellen Jameson, Kitt's niece, shares a story passed down from generation to generation affirming that children of differing eras still have much in common when it comes to enthusiasm, excitement, and anticipation during the Christmas season:

"Here's a little but beautiful story that my grandfather (Foster Jameson) told to me in the late 1970's while I was living at my Aunt Kitt's home in Friendship. Foster and his cousin, Sumner Whitney, were staying at Aunt Kitt's home during Christmas. Sent up to bed in the front bedroom facing the main street, they were looking out the window at the snow falling on Christmas Eve. As they watched, the stagecoach pulled up and the driver, wearing a buffalo robe, walked up to the house with a large package. As my grandfather told me, the two cousins looked at each other wide-eyed and thought, 'no one could tell them that was not Santa Claus.'"

"Many times I would go up to that same room and window on a snowy evening, imagining what it must have been like to see such a beautiful sight. The story is particularly special to me as it was told with

the same wide-eyed wonder and smile on my grandfather's face that must have been present on that Christmas Eve."[5]

Passing Kitt's home, we are very conscious of the great welcoming front porch. Ellen shares another story, this time about Aunt Kitt's porch: "One day while visiting Aunt Kitt at Fieldcrest, I asked her what the two large hooks were on the porch ceiling. She told me that they belonged to the porch swing that Joe (her fiancée) had made for her, and that if I went down into the barn I would find it. She also mentioned that, 'a lot of sparking took place on that swing.' I couldn't wait to get back to the house! I dragged that porch swing up out of the barn and hung it up all by myself, straw mattress and all! And, of course, each and every time I used it I would think of her story. Did I mention that she was a little misty-eyed when she told me?"[6]

Kitt's sense of humor is exposed in the following episode. It seems that Kitt in her latter years was visiting Elden and Beulah Cook. As they commented on how nice she looked, she responded, "The thicker the fog, the nicer I look."

Friendship homes filled with love and memories; memories of devotion to family and country; memories revealing the steadfast character of our ancestors.

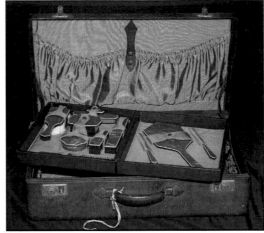

Pat Havener's suitcase from Aunt Kitt.

Photo by Polly Jones

Kitt's window boxes, still beautiful in the fall of 2006.

Photo by Elaine Lang Cornett

Aunt Kitt's Pumpkin Bread

1 can pumpkin
4 eggs
1 cup cooking oil
2/3 cup cold water
3-1/3 cups flour
2 tsp. soda
1 tsp. cinnamon
1 tsp. nutmeg
1-1/2 tsp. salt
3 cups sugar

Mix sugar, pumpkin, eggs, oil and water well.
Sift and add dry ingredients.
Makes 2 large or 3 smaller loaves.
Bake in 350° oven for 1 hour or longer, testing *done* with a cake tester.

Kitt Jameson. *Photo courtesy of Jameson family collection*

14 *The Nellie G. Davis House* By Marilyn Lash

Proceeding south through Friendship village on Harbor Road (Rte. 97), the fifth house on the left past Wallace's Market is locally known as the Nellie Davis house, so named for the woman who called it home for nearly one hundred and two years. Built by Dr. and Mrs. Jason Walker,[1] the stately residence was constructed in the 1860s and is flanked by homes of a similar vintage. Dr. Walker and his wife, Irene, moved from the town of Union and resided in East Friendship in the Moses Orne house while their new home in Friendship village was being built.

The Walker's lived in Friendship for a period of up to twelve years, during eight of which Dr. Walker practiced medicine in the town.[2] Prior to her marriage to Jason Walker, Irene Walker had been the widow of another physician and so was in possession of the various implements and instruments her late husband had used in his practice of the healing arts. It wasn't until after marrying Irene that Jason Walker took up the medical profession as his life's calling, and there is some question as to whether he had ever actually studied medicine or based his choice of profession on the convenience presented by his wife's inheritance of her late husband's medical paraphernalia.

The first floor of

the house was furnished with a kitchen, summer kitchen, front parlor, dining room, and front entry hall and stairway that lead to the second floor where three bedrooms and an open chamber were located. The third floor consisted of a single large room. In the attached barn were two stalls, a chicken coop and, a two-seater privy. The present layout of the house has changed little from the original but for the inclusion of inside plumbing and the conveniences it provides.

The well for the Walker home was dug by a local man, Alex Brasier, who was reportedly well known hereabouts as a character. At some point during the digging, in order to hasten the progress of the project, Mr. Brasier lowered himself into the partially dug hole to light off a stick of dynamite. He then climbed out of the hole to wait for the pending explosion, which failed to materialize. After waiting some time, he again descended into the hole, arriving just in time for the tardy detona-

Nellie G. Davis house

Photo by Elaine Lang Cornett

Elijah Davis silhouette
Courtesy of the Jameson family collection

tion, which miraculously caused him no serious injury but, understandably, left him in somewhat of a state of nervous distress.[3]

While the Walkers were in residence in their new home, Elijah Davis and his young wife, Miranda (Thomas) Davis, both natives of Friendship, were living with Miranda's parents, Jesse and Eleanor (Lawry) Thomas, in a portion of their house at the end of the present-day Tamarack Road next to Blackfish Cove, the property currently owned by Wadsworth Owen. In 1872 Dr. and Mrs. Walker sold their home to Elijah and Miranda, and a residency of Davises began in the home that would last for the next 110 years.

Born in 1839, Elijah Davis was the third of four children of Emery and Elmira (Morton) Davis. Their firstborn, a daughter, died while still a child, and in 1844, the year her fourth child was born, Elijah's mother also passed away. Emery remarried within a few years, and with his new wife, Mary (Cushman) Genthner Davis, a widow from Bremen who had a son two years younger than Elijah, the couple added four more children to their collective family, bringing the total number of surviving children in their brood to eight.[4]

Elijah had embarked on his first career, that of fisherman, at the age of six when he began fishing with his father, Emery, and learning what would become one of his future vocations. Elijah and Miranda married in 1863 during the Civil War, when many other young men were enlisting, including Elijah's younger brother, Emery Jr., and his older brother, Washington, who would not survive the war. Elijah, however, had stayed at home to work and support his family in the fishing trade.

In October 1868 Elijah and Miranda were blessed with the arrival of a daughter, Elmira, known as "Mima" or "Mimie,"[5] who would be an only child for twelve years until sister Nellie G. arrived on December 29 in the year 1880.[6] At some point during these years, Elijah changed professions from that of fisherman to "smacker," owning and operating two lobster smacks[7] during his lifetime, the

Mimie Davis and the *Nellie G. Davis*, that he operated between Boston, Portland, Friendship, and ports in Nova Scotia. He continued to go smacking until a few years before his death at the age of seventy-six, passing away on the morning of Christmas, 1916.[8]

When Elijah's and Miranda's oldest daughter "Mima" was grown, she married the boy next door, Sherman Tecumseh Jameson, the son of Francis and Ruby (Thompson) Jameson, who lived in the neighboring house on the north side of the Davis home, and in 1897 the couple had a son, Foster. When Mima, who was much loved for her easygoing, warm, and friendly nature was overtaken by illness, it first was thought that her malady might have been caused by contaminated well water. A horse had been tied up in front of the Davis family home next to the well, and it was suspected that Mima's illness could be the result of the fouling of the well water by the culprit horse. As a result, the well was condemned, and a second well was dug behind the house as a precaution. However, Mima's illness was not caused by fetid water but, rather, by *Mycobacterium tuberculosis*. In 1901 Mima succumbed to the disease.[9]

When Nellie reached adulthood, she chose a career over marriage, and although she would never have any of her own, she would have a significant influence in the lives of hundreds of children. In 1899 Nellie accepted a one-term position as teacher at the school on Friendship Long Island, "testing the waters," as it were, of a teaching career. Her father, Elijah, would row her to the island each morning and back to the mainland at the end of the school day. Nellie must have enjoyed the work for, following the term, she left Friendship for

Elijah and Miranda Davis in front of the house.   *Photo courtesy of the Jameson family collection*

Nellie Davis in 1921

Photo courtesy of Jameson family collection

the village of Kents Hill and the Maine Wesleyan Seminary and Female College to study to become a teacher, graduating in 1901. She would also later study at the Farmington Normal School, a predecessor of what is today the University of Maine at Farmington.

Nellie's first teaching job, following her graduation, was in the Ulmer District of South Cushing in the spring of 1902. In the fall of the same year she was the school-marm at the Goose River School in Friendship, and for the following year and a half Nellie taught at Friendship's Hatchet Cove school. Over the next dozen years, from 1904 to 1916, Nellie was the school mistress at Pleasant Point in Cushing, at Union's Nye District, again at Goose River in Friendship, in Woolwich, on Chebeague Island in Casco Bay, at Edes Falls in Naples, at Conway Center, New Hampshire,[10] in Edgecomb, in East Friendship, in East Readfield, at Leed's Center, at Dixfield Grammar School, at South Gardiner, in Brunswick, and then back in Cushing. When her father, Elijah, passed in 1916, Nellie stopped teaching and cared for her mother, Miranda, until after her death in 1919. Resuming her career in 1920, Nellie continued to teach until her retirement in 1947, which found her at Minot Corner in Poland, Maine.

Nellie's abilities as a teacher and disciplinarian were apparently highly regarded, as attested to in a letter of recommendation written in 1914 by W.S. McNamara, superintendent of schools in the Mexico and Dixfield Union School District. "Miss Davis came to Dixfield when the school was in very poor condition owing to the incapacity of former teachers, the discipline being especially poor," wrote superintendent McNamara. "In one term she brought order out of chaos and before the end of the school year her room was in excellent condition... Miss Davis is well liked by pupils, parents and school officials... I consider her an excellent teacher in every respect and should be very sorry to have her go elsewhere."

When Nellie taught in schools outside of Friendship, room and board had to be paid in whatever town she was employed. A letter dated July 4, 1915, from the office of the superintendent of schools in Brunswick informs Nellie that, "If you accept this school... an excellent boarding place may be secured very near the schoolhouse with Mrs. Jennie Newell. The price of board will be $3.00 per week if you remain all the time...We could not pay more than $10.00."[11] Yet in spite of the meager pay and the expense of maintaining the family home that was Nellie's alone to bear after her mother's death in 1919, Nellie was always faithful to provide money for college books for her sister's grandchildren and great-grandchildren, and during the Great Depression it was rumored that she quietly contributed funds to help those in need.

The young woman who had left the familiarity of family and home to pursue a college education and a career that would take her to sundry locations in an era when few young people would have been so adventurous, returned to the family homestead in Friendship when she retired from the profession of teaching that in all spanned forty-eight years, and there she made her home for the remainder of her life.[12] She was active in the Friendship United Methodist Church, faithfully attending services, and was a member of a button club. Club members would collect and

Nellie's house and barn in fall 2006.

Photo by Elaine Lang Cornett

swap buttons of all shapes, sizes and descriptions, some rare. She always kept her large home in excellent repair, a fact much appreciated by its present owners, who say that the home's present condition provides evidence that it was never abused and was always well maintained.[13] Nellie lived another thirty-five years after retirement, passing away on August 4, 1982,[14] fewer than five months before her 102nd birthday.

In 1984 Nellie's house was sold by her heirs to Edmund and Paula Turgeon, who owned it briefly and who apparently never resided at the property. On October 13, 1986, the present owners, Larry Jennings and his wife, Ann Alvis, purchased the home, and the following summer opened it as The Summer House Bed-and-Breakfast.[15]

The Alvis-Jenningses tell a story of their arrival in Friendship in the summer of 1987, the first summer they opened the house as a B&B.

Friends and Neighbors

Nellie Davis, born in 1880,[1] and Katharyn "Kitt" Jameson, born in 1882,[2] grew up in neighboring homes that sat only a few dozen feet from one another. The two neighbors related by marriage (Nellie's older sister, Elmira, married Kitt's brother, Sherman) would each attend and graduate from college in an era when the formal education of most would end at the eighth grade. Neither would ever marry, both would inherit and make their homes in their family homesteads for the remainder of their lives, both were being cared for at the Fieldcrest

Nellie's graduation photo.
Courtesy Jameson family collection

Nursing Home at the end of their lives,[3] and both are buried in the Old Village Cemetery behind the Methodist Church in Friendship with but one headstone separating in death the lifelong neighbors.[4]

[1] Beth Delano, *Stone Reunions: A comprehensive look at the cemeteries of Friendship, Maine* (Camden, Maine: Penobscot Press, 2005) p. 87.
[2] A visit to the Old Village Cemetery.
[3] Patricia Jameson Havener, interview, Friendship, Me, March 2007.
[4] A visit to the Old Village Cemetery.

Nellie's friend and neighbor, Kitt Jameson.
Courtesy Jameson family collection

Their daughter, Sydney, was only two weeks old at the time and was sick. They were acquainted with almost no one in town with the exception of the Methodist pastor, Richard Parker, who supplied them with the name of a doctor in Rockland. They waited in the car for three hours to see the physician, who told them the infant had a cold and to "get a vaporizer." No stores selling the required equipment were open, and the good reverend said, "I can find one for you," and within three hours five people had shown up at the house with vaporizers. Apparently, the new homeowners felt Friendship had lived up to its name.

Also soon after taking-up residence, the Alvis-Jenningses were introduced to that form of the English language known as "down cast." In an attempt to get to know some of his neighbors better, Larry Jennings joined in a house painting party at the home across the street from the new B&B. When he came home for lunch he said to his wife, Ann, "I can't understand a thing anybody's saying over there. When they say something to me I just nod and say 'yes.' They probably think I'm a moron."

Nellie's grandnephew, William Jameson, late of Waldoboro (Foster's son, Mima's grandson), made a gift to Ann and Larry of Nellie's college diploma, which is a treasured keepsake proudly displayed. The piano that once belonged to Nellie but that following her death was donated to the Methodist Church and was later purchased by a local resident, has made its way back to Nellie's house, and Ann and Larry would be pleased to locate other former items from the home.

The Summer House Bed-and-Breakfast was operated during the summers of 1987 through 1989. Since then it has been rented out from time to time when the Alvis-Jennings family isn't in residence. Although Larry, Ann, and Sydney live in Florida the majority of the time, they love their home in Friendship, deeply appreciating its heritage and thinking of it themselves as "Nellie's house".

Nellie's Date Roll-Up Cookies

2 c. brown sugar, packed
3/4 c. margarine
1 t. soda
1 t. cream of tartar
1/4 t. salt
2-1/2 c. flour
2 eggs
1 t. vanilla

Filling:
Cook 1-1/2 c. chopped dates with 1/2 c. sugar and 3/4 c. water ---till it thickens. Add 1 t. orange extract & 3/4 c. chopped nuts.

Make dough and chill. Roll out small amounts of dough, spread with filling, roll up and chill. Slice in rounds. Place on cookie sheet. Bake in a 400-degree oven 7 to 8 minutes.

15 *The Thomas Benner House* By Alice Benner

The Thomas Benner house was built in the early 1900s by Thomas Alden Benner (1863-1944). In addition to the main house, there were several outbuildings, including a large barn and a carriage house. The carriage house has since been renovated to a small home. The main house had intricate gingerbread trim and featured stained-glass windows. Thomas Benner was a farmer, odd-job laborer, and carpenter who built several houses in Friendship in addition to his own. Similarities in design can be seen in many of these houses, among them those presently the homes of Arnold and Alice Benner, Lynn Meyer, and Alan Simmons.

Thomas was a bachelor until he was 53, when he married Katherine

Heck Neubig. They brought up their two sons, Herbert and Thomas Jr., as well as Katherine's son, Jack, in this house.

Thomas and Katherine took in boarders, and one of the groups who boarded there was the men who were working to string the wires to bring electricity to the town circa 1927. They turned on the electricity in this house and the Benners had lights the night before it was turned on for the rest of the town.[1]

Many stories have been told of Thomas Benner's great strength and endurance. It is said that when a wagon carrying an 800-pound chest broke its axle under Cook's Hill, Thomas lifted the wagon, chest and all, while it was repaired.[2]

When the water main was dug for Elmer Jameson's water system in the late 1890s, Thomas Benner was one of the workers. He dug by hand 100 feet of water line four feet deep each day.[3]

On a bet, Thomas was challenged to saw four cords of wood with a bucksaw. The wood was in four-foot lengths, and he sawed each

Thomas Benner house circa 1920. Thomas Benner is at left on the porch. The young boys at far right are Thomas Benner Jr. and Herbert Benner.

Photo courtesy of the Benner family collection

stick twice. His brother, Elmer Benner, sharpened the saws for him. He completed the task in seven hours and 45 minutes.[4]

On November 11, 1922, an article appeared in the *Lewiston Evening Journal* describing the clamming industry in Bremen. "Eight bushels a day is a pretty good catch but there is a retired clam digger in Friendship, Tom Benner, who, about 30 years ago, established a record. It was 18 bushels in a tide. It was a never-to-be-forgotten sight to see Tom in action on the clam flats. He forged ahead like a tractor and behind him the flats looked like a ploughed field."[5]

Thomas and Katherine's son Herbert and his wife, Anne, brought up their eight children in this house. For easier maintenance, Herbert changed the look of the house in the 1950s by removing the gingerbread in favor of the porch as it looks now. Herbert's son Wayne and his wife, Diana, are presently living in the house.

Merganser by George Huey, Benner family heirloom.   *Photo by Carol Hoch*

Carved Duck

Two brothers, Herbert and Thomas Benner Jr., solved a problem some time back when they were given a string of duck tollers by George Huey. George Huey (1886-1946) was a native son of Friendship who carved decoys. His carved mergansers are described this way in *The Great Book of Wildfowl Decoys*: "Huey's mergansers were the best on the coast of Maine."[1] They decided the best plan was to divide the tollers evenly, but because there was an odd number, and in order to keep things fair, Thomas cut one of the carved ducks in half. You might ask, "Who got the head and who got the tail?" The answer would be, "Neither." Thomas cut the decoy from head to tail as skillfully as you please, and both brothers had a fine specimen to mount on their walls— a half-hull, if you will, of a George Huey.

A half Huey is better than none, but in today's auction market, a George Huey in good condition brings between $5,000 - $10,000 or more. Check your attic for just such a possible hidden treasure!

[1] Joe Engers (General Editor), *The Great Book of Wildfowl Decoys* (San Diego: Thunder Bay Press, Inc., 1990), p. 28.

Thomas Benner house circa 1930, *Field Day* parade.   *Photo courtesy of Marguerite C. Sylvester*

Benner family at work.   *Courtesy of the Friendship library from the Chubb Patch collection*

Benner family at home.   *Courtesy of the Benner family collection*

16 *The Walter H. Wotton House* By Patricia Winchenbach

Sherman and Paul Wotton in front of the Wotton house circa 1908.

Photo courtesy of Margaret Wotton Gagnon

Walter H. Wotton House in the 2006.

Photo courtesy of Margaret Wotton Gagnon

Just south of the center of town on Harbor Road, and situated on the highest point of land in the village of Friendship, sits the Walter H. Wotton home. Its location afforded a perfect view of the town's harbor and Davis Point, where the Jameson and Wotton business was located. During the days of steamships, this was the stopping point for boats hailing from Boston and Portland bringing in fresh materials and food supplies for the folks living on the islands and along the coast, as well as the latest news from the rest of the world.

Set back and graciously surrounded by groves of lilacs and *Rosa rugosa* hedges, Walter Wotton's house stands as beautiful today as it was the day he gifted it to his lovely new bride, Mary Etta, in 1900. The house is inviting with its wraparound porch, edged by hourglass-shaped railings, and the gingerbread trimming the rooflines defines the comfort and elegance of this home. Small perennial gardens of snowdrops and hyacinth appear in the early spring, and 100-year-old rosebushes bloom deep magenta in the summer.

Inside, the rooms are spacious with high ceilings and elongated Victorian style windows. The staircase in the hallway is lined with 43 balusters, hand turned and sold by Levitt Storer for a total cost of $3.01 or 7 cents apiece. In a little brown book, Walter made a note of the total cost of the house, $1699.96.

About six years after moving into the home, and coincidentally during the very year of Friendship's centennial anniversary, 1907, Mary Etta gave birth to twin boys. Margaret Gagnon, Walter's granddaughter and current owner of the home, surmises that Walter, at 43 years old, had probably just about given up the prospect of having his own family, and suddenly, here he was with two sons! He was elated as news traveled down the coast and letters of congratulation arrived from as far away as Boston. His boys, Paul and Sherman, would grow up to be mechanical wizards, always designing one thing or another. When the boys were 19 years old, they each decided to enter a science magazine matchcraft contest. Over an eight-month period, Sherman built a "snappy roadster" made of 2,600 safety matches, and Paul, in six months' time, assembled 2,200 matches into a miniature radio set. Both boys won a second-place prize of $75.00.[1] Walter recognized his boys' talents and decided that upon their graduations, they should attend the General Electric Apprentice course in Lynn, Massachusetts. Both men spent their entire working years there, but upon retirement they returned to Friendship.

Sherman, Margaret's father, moved back into the home following the death of Mary Etta Wotton in 1968. He used his building skills to historically restore the house and outer building to their original state. In 2000 the home was passed on to Margaret, who has strived to maintain its original beauty.

Although only three generations lived in this house, what is remarkable about the Walter H. Wotton homestead is more than just the house itself. It is the multitude of stories that happened long before the house was ever built, but which have been preserved within its walls all these years, waiting to be retold. One of those stories is about Lorenzo Wotton, Walter's father. He left his home here in Friendship for the first time in his life at the age of 25 to fight for the Union Army during the Civil War. He was wounded at Port Hudson, Louisiana. Fortunately, but unlike so many others, he made it back home to Friendship and to his wife, Suzanna, and his one-year-old

Itemized ledger with the cost of the Walter H. Wotton house.

Photo courtesy of Margaret Wotton Gagnon

daughter, Martha. Five more children followed, the first of which was Walter. Lorenzo's original military discharge papers were recently found folded and tucked safely away in the attic.

When reading through the historic documentation found here in the house, names begin to ring familiar: Wottons, Brewsters, Bradfords, Thompsons, Jamesons, and Aldens. It doesn't take long to realize that these are not merely stories of the Wotton family, but, rather, they are stories of

The Walter H. Wotton house under construction. *Photo courtesy of Margaret Wotton Gagnon*

The Walter H. Wotton house circa 1910 *Photo courtesy of Margaret Wotton Gagnon*

Wotton twins Sherman, left and Paul, right, with their parents in the car in front of the house in 1914. *Photo courtesy of Margaret Wotton Gagnon*

a settlement named Meduncook that later became a town called Friendship.

In 1900 Walter and Mary Etta brought to their new home what was obviously dear to them, their families' historical records, certificates, and photographs. During their lifetimes, they added more documentation. These records date as far back as to William Bradford, governor of the Plymouth Bay Colony and signer of the Mayflower Compact. Walter H. Wotton was a ninth generation direct descendent of William Bradford. In all those generations there are far too many stories to tell in this short book, however, *if* this house could talk, what stories it could tell indeed.

Decorative gingerbread railing on porch.
Photo by Margaret Wotton Gagnon

The hand-turned bannister at the base of the main staircase.
Photo by Margaret Wotton Gagnon

Lupines in Margaret's garden.
Photo by Margaret Wotton Gagnon

Wotton Twins Win Matchcraft Contest

By Linda S. DeRosa

Sherman Wotton with his matchstick Roadster.
Photo courtesy of Margaret Wotton Gagnon

Matchstick roadster.
Photo courtesy of Margaret Wotton Gagnon

Matchstick radio.
Photo courtesy of Margaret Wotton Gagnon

What was happening on December 1, 1925, in Friendship that was directly connected to Liberty Matches, a set of twins, and the Experimenter Publishing Company in New York City? I'll tell you what. An important matchcraft contest was launched by the *Science and Invention Magazine* published monthly in New York City, to run for 12 months through December 1, 1926. The twins were Sherman F. and his brother, Paul R. Wotton, sons of Walter H. Wotton in Friendship.

A fall issue of *Science and Invention Magazine* sparked their interest, and both 19-year-olds took on the challenge to make an award-winning item out of common safety matches. There were special instructions as to how to pack and mail the entries: "Make sure first that your model is constructed strongly enough to withstand severe shocks. Then, before you send us the model, after you have it packed as well as you know how, throw it up almost to the ceiling and let it come down on the floor. Open up the box and see if the model is not damaged. Only after such a test can you know that the model will arrive safely."[1] I wonder if Paul and Sherman tested their packing skills this way after spending six months and eight months, respectively, on completing their models.

Paul completed his radio set after six months of endeavor between school hours and during his spare time and using 2,200 matches. Sherman took eight months and used 2,600 matches to create a snappy roadster complete with springs, a tie rod, bumpers, and a working steering wheel. Both of the young men won the November second-place prize of $75.00, as written about in the November 1926 issue of *Science and Invention*.

The May 8, 1927, issue of the *Portland Sunday Telegram* also ran this story in the section "Latest News and Feature Stories from Among Maine Cities and Towns". In the piece it notes, "Both lads intend to go to college but will not follow up their art of fashioning articles of matches."[2]

1. Science and Invention, November 1926, pp. 605 & 607.
2. Portland Sunday Telegram & Sunday Press Herald, May 8, 1927, Section A, p. 4.

17 *Sherman Tecumseh Jameson House* By Celia Lash Briggs

On the rise of land above the harbor, two houses sit diagonally facing one another across the main road. To the east is a charming Victorian laced with gingerbread trim, and to the west is a stately home graced by a porch and topped with a Palladian window. These two houses were built by the partners who owned the Jameson and Wotton Store and the steamboat wharf at the harbor, which were the pulse of the town. From their high perch, the entrepreneurs could observe comings and goings by land and by sea.

Sherman Tecumseh Jameson was a fifth-generation Friendship native and son of a Civil War veteran. On February 24, 1894, he married a local girl, Elmira (Mima) Davis, daughter of Elijah and Miranda Thomas Davis. Soon after the turn of the century, the Jamesons began work on their new home. They had been living in Tom Benner's house while constructing their own next door. They purchased a lot from Walter Wotton that was located across the road from his new Victorian. Walter had bought the land with a small house on it for his wife's sister and her husband, Ollie and Levi Noyes. He had moved the little house to the lot next to his toward the village.

There was no electricity in Friendship at the time that the house was under construction, but Sherm went ahead and had it wired and plumbed

Sherman Tecumseh Jameson house circa 1915.

Photo courtesy of Jameson family collection

in anticipation of enjoying future conveniences. Until power was brought to town, the indoor plumbing operated by gravity feed from a wooden tank in back of the house. This was filled from a large elevated wooden tank just down the road that was part of the town water company owned by Elmer Jameson I.[1]

Sherman Tecumseh Jameson as a young man.

Photo courtesy Jameson family collection

Sherm and Mima had one son, Foster Davis, born on December 16, 1897. Mima died a few years later, and Sherm later married Sarah Kilmer, who was from a family that summered on Davis Point.

The following excerpt is taken from the journals of Foster's son, William Jameson: "For some reason secret marriages were the thing that year. My father and mother (Agnes Newburn) had a double wedding with Myron and Edith (Murphy) Neal in the front room of my grandparents' home, the house I was born in the following June. The minister who had been told the ceremony was to be a secret, came down the street in his old clothes so the neighbors would think he was just making a casual call at the house. I was a year old when we moved to Waldoboro."[2]

Sherman Tecumseh Jameson house, left and the Walter H. Wotton house, right.

Photo courtesy Jameson family collection

A William Jameson Memoir

Back in the 1940s I spent several summers working for my grandfather, Sherman Jameson. He had been a lobster dealer for years in Friendship and went from island to island in Muscongus Bay buying lobsters from the fishermen. His lobster smack, the *Foster D*, was a familiar sight in the bay for over fifty years. We had a lot of time to talk while waiting for fishermen to finish hauling, and he told me many stories about the Friendship area. One of these stories had to do with a race he sailed in when he was a boy – a race won of course by the boat he was on, the sloop *Clara Benner*. As I remember the story the *Clara Benner* had trimmed everything in Friendship, so when the Rockland Yacht Club invited all boats to enter a regatta on September 5, 1878, his uncle Webb Thompson, who was one of the owners of the *Clara Benner*, decided to see what she could do in a yacht race. He took my grandfather, then a boy of fourteen, along with Will Hamlin, as crew. Will Hamlin, a sail maker by trade, had made the sails for the *Clara Benner* when she was built at the Cobb wharf far up at the head of Friendship Harbor.

The race was sailed over a five-mile course in Rockland Harbor so that spectators on the wharves could have a good view. Two boats from the Rockland Yacht Club had been taking first and second place in the races for a couple of years These two, the *Nettie Pendleton*, owned by C.H. Pendleton, and the *Maud*, owned by S. H. Boynton were out to beat each other and didn't realize that the *Clara Benner* was winning until it was too late. After the race, the captain of the *Nettie Pendleton* allowed as how the Friendship boat wouldn't have won if he hadn't been intent on beating the *Maud*. Captain Webb retorted that if that was the way he felt about it, why not go back out and settle the matter then and there. Webb was not unaware that the wind had freshened from the southwest during the afternoon and that the stronger the breeze, the better the *Clara Benner* sailed. My grandfather said "Tillson's Wharf was black with people when we went out for our private race, and this time we really trounced the *Nettie Pendleton*.

The Friendship crew went home with first prize, a silver fruit bowl, and the joy of having beaten the best boats in the area. My grandfather always claimed that the publicity from that race interested people in Friendship sloops for the first time. From then on the boat shops of the town had plenty of orders. As more sloops were built it became the custom to take the fastest of the year's lot to Rockland to show people there what a Friendship sloop could do. In 1884 a Friendship sloop won the Rockland Regatta, and the next year it was decided to have a yacht race in Friendship as part of a big Fourth of July celebration. That race was different from the present ones. That time not all the sloops in the area entered. Evidently, boat owners didn't want to race then if they didn't have a good chance of winning.[1]

[1] Jameson Family History, from the collection of Patricia Jameson Havener

The minister was Ernest E. Small, pastor of the Baptist church.

Reading on in William's journals we find this recollection: "One of my early remembrances of visiting my grandparents was of waiting for my grandfather to come home from the store (Jameson and Wotton) in the late afternoon. He took a large oval metal lunch bucket with a part that could be put on the stove to warm up the coffee in it. The metal cup slid over a cylindrical part on the top of the lunch bucket. When Grandpa came in and set his lunch bucket down, I took the cup off and always found a couple of peppermints or other pieces of candy."[3]

Thurmond and Ivy Gould purchased the house in the mid-1900s, and Ivy, who is 90 years old, still lives there. She has kept the interior much the same as it was when first built. The original oak woodwork surrounding the doors and fireplaces still glows as it did when new.

Four generations of Jamesons: William Sherman Jameson in front; left to right, Foster Davis Jameson, Francis Gracia Jameson, and Sherman Tecumseh Jameson. *Photo courtesy of Jameson family collection*

Sherman Tecumseh Jameson house in Winter 2007.

Photo by Victor Motyka

IV Jameson/Davis Point

Photo by Elaine Lang Cornett

18 *The Davis Houses* By Priscilla Wilder Ambrose

Down the hill from Friendship village at the top of the Davis Point promontory, which creates Friendship harbor on the east and Hatchet Cove to the west, stands a cluster of 19th-century homes. All these houses were built by various members of the Davis family during the 1800s when they moved in from Friendship Long Island.

When one reads Doctor William Hahn's *History of Friendship*, and the vast quantity of additional Hahn notes not included in the book but compiled by Mary Carlson, one can grasp the history of early families that made Friendship their home. The Davises, for instance, still very much part of the community today, started their presence here by settling on Friendship Long Island in the mid-18th century, as did many of the other early families. The settlers were mostly of English origin, descendants of the Plymouth Pilgrims who came here for the better fishing opportunities.[1]

The islands were closer to the fishing banks and provided better protection from possible Indian attacks. Those who lived on the islands were necessarily farmers as much as they were fishermen, enabling them to be self-sufficient. The Davises held forth on Long Island until the beginning of the 19th century, when they began to emigrate to the mainland. Over a span of one hundred years there were six Davis homes built in the neighborhood just above and at the northern end of what we now call the "Davis Point Loop."

All of these homes are in use today. One of them has been moved to another location farther down the point. Each of the houses is different from the other, and all are architecturally impressive. As a group they represent a significant and historic group of 19th-century homes.

The first Davis house in this mainland neighborhood was built in 1835 by Joshua Davis, son of Bradford. Three generations of Joshua's

The Bradford Davis house. *Photo by Linda S. DeRosa*

family branch (Joshua, Silas, Lauriston) inhabited this Cape with extended ells and two designs of gingerbread into the second half of the 20th century. The house, as do all the others, overlooks the harbor. Early post-cards and photographs show "fish flakes," cod drying on platforms, in the fields below and all around the house.[2]

Bradford Davis, father of Joshua, came into the mainland from Long Island when the two of them purchased most of the land on the Davis Point peninsula and built the first house in the lower loop area at least by 1838 (accounts differ). Bradford had started a brick factory in Friendship and built his little red brick house as an early example of this medium. The house continues to be occupied and enjoyed today as it sits at the top of the hill overlooking the harbor.

Joshua's brother Emery Davis, second generation to emigrate in from the island, and the seventh of ten siblings, built his house in 1840, a farmhouse Cape, across from his father and somewhat down the street from his older brother. We know much history of this house,

The Joshua Davis homestead. *Photo by Linda S. DeRosa*

The Emery Davis house. *Photo courtesy of Jameson family collection*

thanks in part to Emery's daughter, Amanda, who saved letters from her correspondents during the era of the Civil War, and to Courtney MacLachlan who discovered these letters a century and a half later and presented them in a remarklable book entitled, *The Amanda Letters*.[3]

Emery himself has quite a history as a fisherman, farmer, soldier, family man, and townsman. His name comes up repeatedly in Captain Cook's Meduncook Plantation Record book (1762-1899). Perhaps the most colorful reference is the account of the destruction by torch of Emery's schooner, *Magnolia,* here in our own waters in 1864.[4]

It is stirring to encounter this Emery Davis house, solidly positioned at the corner of the loop when one is heading down to the wharves or around the loop, and to ponder its amazing but little considered 19th-century history. And still, there's more to come.

Robert Mitchell Armstrong, first generation of an enduring and vital seasonal family, purchased the Emery Davis home in 1899. Armstrong with others had founded a YMCA camp on Crotch Island and needed accommodation for the families of the campers. The Sea View Hotel was thus founded for Camp Durell's families and other guests. After the hotel closed during the First World War, guests no longer came, but the Armstrong family proliferated and continue there now into five generations.

Moses Kenney married Charlotte Davis, sister of Joshua and Emery. Moses and Charlotte built a house for their son, Bradford Kenney, in 1868. This handsome Victorian clapboard house is on Harbor Road, the only house in all of the five 19th-century Davis homes remaining in the cluster today to be occupied on a year around basis in 2007. Bradford Kenney was a cousin and a neighbor of Amanda Davis just a stone's throw away. He and his wife, Sophie, are frequently mentioned in Amanda's letters to and from some of their other cousins in Warren and on the Civil War battlefields or in the wartime hospitals. Their son, Elmer, was lost at sea at the age of 22, and left his wife, Harriet, to look after the house and her father-in-law, now a widower after Sophie's death.

The Bradford Kenney house.

Photo by Polly Jones

VIEW OF DAVIS POINT, FRIENDSHIP ME. 24

The Foster Davis house, now located on Davis Point Loop.

From the collection of Robert S. Lash, Jr.

Hattie, or Hat as she came to be called, the young widow, supported herself and her father-in-law by working as a sail seamstress across the road at Wilbur Morse's bustling boat yard down on the shore. When Wilbur's wife died and Bradford Kenney died, Wilbur married Hat, who became a Morse family favorite while living in another important house in the neighborhood.[5]

A third generation of Davis house builders in this early neighborhood, Everin Davis, built his home across Harbor Road from Emery, his father, in the 1870s. High on the hill overlooking the harbor, this house at the time, as well as the others, had very few trees to occupy the view and only one wharf down below on the water. Ev Davis retains a special place in local lore. He rescued Mrs. B.B. Jameson when B.B. backed his car off the Jameson and Wotton Wharf at the bottom of his street in 1923.

A sixth house in the Davis group was built in the late 19th century by Foster Davis across the Loop Road from his father, Emery, and almost directly in front of his Grandfather Bradford's house. How such an unfortunate positioning could occur is anybody's guess, but it remained there until 1967, when it was moved further down the Loop Road to become a dwelling for members of the ever-proliferating Armstrong family. Five of the six Davis houses discussed here are now owned and used on a seasonal basis in the summer community that has developed and endured over the last century in the Davis Point Loop area.

It should be important to recognize these homes as a unique family cluster of dwellings from more than a century ago, but few of us realize today when whizzing by in our modern cars on modern roads, that in all three directions we are passing right through the center of the old Davis neighborhood. Do we ever consider this? Mostly not, it seems. How intriguing it is to think about that tight-knit family community, the horse and buggies, the horse-drawn sleighs in winter, the whole picture as it unfolds through the passage of time. What history we have right here in our midst!

19 *The Joshua Davis Homestead* By Bonnie Davis Micue

It is the human story that makes a house a home. In the case of the Joshua Davis homestead information herein is from family recollection.

Sarah Bradford, a surviving daughter of Joshua and Hannah Bradford, married John Davis, and they moved to Friendship Long Island where they established their household, which would grow to seven children. Their youngest son, Bradford, together with his son Joshua bought the entire tract of land shown on the charts as Jameson's Point and known locally as Davis Point.

Joshua Davis erected a house, whose eaves were distinguished by what was referred to as "Norwegian overhang" (gingerbread trim), on the harbor side of the hill in 1835, and that house still stands overlooking Friendship harbor and the islands. Bradford, who owned and ran a brick factory, built a brick house across the roadway from Joshua's house, and the two Davises split the land in a deed dated April 11, 1838. Family history places Joshua's house with its distinguishing gingerbread trim as being the longest existing house on the point.

Joshua Davis married Phoebe Mahoney, and together they had three children, Silas (who would inherit the house), Samuel (who inherited the Daniel Davis house), and George, who died while still a boy. The story goes that no one ever caught Phoebe Davis asleep. Her husband,

Joshua Davis house in late Summer 2006.

Photo by Polly Jones

Joshua Davis house as it looked in the 1890s, while occupied by Silas & Nancy Davis (with Minnie)   *Photo courtesy of Davis family collection.*

on the other hand, cherished his rest. When the Confederate raider *Tallahassee* made its swing through Muscongus Bay in 1864 (burning Josh's brother Emery's schooner *Magnolia* in its destructive path), Emery ran to Josh's house to alert him to the fact that the raider was passing through the harbor. The story goes that he rushed into the house yelling for Josh, "The ole *Tallahassee* is here." Josh responded, "Get on back home and leave me to my bed."

The Davises made their living farming, fishing, and shipping. Old photos of the homestead show fish flakes (drying cod) which was then shipped on their own schooner to the West Indies, bringing back molasses to Massachusetts and rum to Maine.

Silas Davis, Josh's second son, spent most of his working life on schooners, including the *Minnie Davis*, named for his oldest daughter. Minnie's mother, Martha Wallace, had been sickly, and Silas hired Nancy Simmons to move off Friendship Long Island to care for her and their young daughter Minnie. After Martha died, Nancy entertained an

Friendship harbor, circa 1950s   *Courtesy of the Friendship library from the Chubb Patch collection*

offer of marriage from a young man on the island, but Silas was not interested in losing her and made her an offer of marriage, which she accepted. They had two children together, Martha born in 1876 and Lauriston born in 1887.

In the spring of 1900 Nancy sickened with pneumonia and died on June first. Silas opened a portion of his back pasture as a graveyard and buried her there, moving the remains of his first wife to join her. So began the Harbor Cemetery. Silas's white monument overlooking the cemetery marks their resting place.

He continued to farm and fish along with his son Lauriston, who as a young child contracted bone tuberculosis and became lame. Silas also began selling off parcels of his father's land. In the 1890s he also contracted with Burnham and Morrill, who built a factory on the shore of Friendship harbor to process clams.

In the early 1910s Lauriston opened a general store across the road from his father's house, and it was there he brought his bride, Elizabeth Eaton, whom he had met at his Uncle Sam's where she was visiting. Their first son, Lauriston Eaton, was born while they lived there.

General store owned and operated by Lauriston B. Davis circa 1913

Photo courtesy of Davis family collection.

Silas died in 1918, and Lauriston and Elizabeth moved across the road into the homestead— the third and fourth generations to live there. Lauriston Eaton remembered clearly the day that electricity came to the house; it was turned on one Christmas Eve. A second son, George Edgar was born after the family had moved into the homestead. The general store was closed, as the needs of the farm took more and more time.

As in days gone by, the family was occupied in various ways of earning a living. In addition to farming and fishing, the father Lauriston also peddled fish throughout the inland communities. Son Lauriston would often accompany his father, first fishing and then delivering. By horse and wagon and later automobile, the two would drive the fish into interior towns such as Jefferson, Burkettville, and Somerville, where they became welcome visitors into the homes to which they brought fresh fish.

By the mid-1930s, farming was giving way to fishing as the major source of family income, and farming held little interest for sons Eaton and Edgar. Both became lobster fishermen and left farming behind. Elizabeth made and sold donuts; her effects at the time of her death included several rolls of silver dimes that she had saved from her donut sales. The wives of the two Lauristons also ran an ice cream parlor from one of the farming sheds, selling Edwards Ice Cream of Rockland fame.

In 1938 Lauriston Eaton married Lois Harkins, and they renovated one end of the house where they lived for several years. Their oldest

View of the Friendship harbor from Joshua Davis homestead

Photo by Linda S. DeRosa

Friendship Harbor

Blue skies, white cumulus clouds
Mirrored in the harbor waters,
Sometimes brilliant,
Sometimes white-capped
As the wind ruffles its surface.
Lobster buoys, multicolored jewels,
Decorate the ocean's wide expanse.
Wooded islands beckon,
"Come, come away and picnic."
Such an awesome sight
At Friendship harbor!

Boats, every size, shape and color,
All neatly facing into the wind,
Add to the striking scene.
Fishermen in yellow oilskins
Maneuver them with precision.
Teens, bold and confident,
Grasp the tillers with familiarity.
Children, totally without fear,
Clamber from bow to stern.
All part of the picture
At Friendship harbor!

Relax to the music of the waves
As they roll up on the shore.
Bathe in the summer sun
As you breathe the salty air.
At night gaze at the full moon
Reflected on the calm waters.
With each dip of the oars
The dark waters gleam fluorescent.
Capture joy and spectacular memories.
Surround yourself with a relaxing peace,
At Friendship harbor!

Marguerite C. Sylvester

child, Norma, was born while they occupied their end of the homestead, the fifth generation to live there. During World War II, Lois was one of the civilian plane spotters, using the advantage of the high location as an observation point.

As the farming days came to an end, some of the sheds and barn were torn down to make room for a new house built by Lauriston for his growing family, which eventually included Blaine, Bonnie, and Kathy. The little house he built there was eventually moved across the point to its present location on the corner of the Elmer Jameson Road and the Harbor Cemetery Road to make room for the house Edgar Davis would build for his family (wife Mildred and children Sonia and Bradford Joshua) next to his childhood home.

Father Lauriston died in 1958; his wife, Elizabeth, remarried to a childhood friend and remained in the house until her death in 1967. Sons Eaton and Edgar had by then each built new homes on the family land. Her husband, Newell Simmons, had retained a life tenancy and when he left the house to live his remaining days with his children, the house passed from the Davis family in 1977 when it was purchased by Connie and Anderson Pace, who brought major structural renovations to the old house.

The Paces sold the house to Joanne and Francis Hatch in 1983 to move into the Rinehart house across the road. Frank Hatch once told Eaton Davis that the house was too cold to spend winters in, although central heating had been added in the form of a warm air furnace. Eaton was highly amused to hear that his boyhood home, which had been heated by coal stoves throughout his father's life there, was unfit for winter habitation.

In 1997 Joanne and Frank Hatch sold the house to Christine Rinehart Basham. This brought the old house into the Armstrong family, which had joined the Davises on the point in 1899 as part of the summer colony that sprang up in Friendship. Current owners Victoria and Arden Lambert are also part of the Armstrong family and continue to be part of the summer colony. The house today has passed from a year-round home into a seasonal "cottage," yet it remains a picturesque landmark with its distinguishing features of "Norwegian overhang" overlooking Friendship harbor.

20   *Jameson & Wotton Wharf*   By James E. & Nina M. Scott

When the Boat Came In

I can hear the steamboat whistle
As I used to years ago
When she came inside the island
Up the harbor, plowing slow.
I can see the folks all hurrying
To the dock down by the shore.
'Twas the day's event of interest
That we wouldn't miss, you know:
That we will ever remember
From our youth of years ago.[1]

Allison M. Watts

Even in the 1940s I can remember the mystique of the old steamboat wharf. As a boy I would go there, sit on the end of the moveable loading ramp for the long-gone steamboat, and fish for flounder and even catch some too. One time I caught so many that when I strung them on the line, the collection was nearly as tall as I was. While Dad was in the Pacific during WWII, Mom would bring us to the cottage on Davis Point for the summer because it was much less expensive than suburban New York. She planted a Victory Garden with vegetables, and

The Jameson and Wotton wharf in 1913.

Photo courtesy of Margaret Wotton Gagnon

we fished from a rowboat for what we could eat and then canned the rest for winter. The wharf was always a place for dreams for a boy. How did it all begin?

Fish warden Fred McLaughlin on Stenger's wharf, George Cushman in dory in foreground.

From the collection of Robert S. Lash, Jr.

On July 15, 1896, Sherman Tecumseh Jameson wrote a request to the Selectmen of Friendship "to extend the Old Davis Wharf by 100 feet into the harbor." Sherm Jameson came into possession of the Old Davis Wharf because he married Elmira (Mima) Davis in 1894. Selectmen C. W. Wotton and John Studley acknowledged the request and by September sent a license to extend the wharf by 100 feet, according to documents held by Patricia Jameson Havener, Sherm's great-granddaughter and family archivist. The motivation for this construction came from Capt. Ed Archibald, who owned the steamboat line from Rockland to Portland. Previously, none of the docks in Friendship had enough deep water at low tide for the steamboat to unload and load passengers and freight. Captain Archibald said to Jameson that if he would lengthen his dock to deep water and reserve space at the end for the steamer when she came in, this would be the exclusive stop in Friendship. Every Tuesday and Thursday the *Silver Star*, later the *Mineola*, and later still the *Monhegan*, would land going northward, and every Wednesday and Friday she would stop going south. Townspeople took the steamer to Portland and beyond. Local products were shipped to market, and visitors from away stepped onto the dock to take advantage of the newly constructed summer hotels: the Argyle Inn on Davis Point and the Seaview Inn just up the hill from the wharf, where their recreational needs were met.

West side of Jameson and Wotton wharf.　　*Photo courtesy of Penobscot Marine Museum*

The *Foster D.*　　*Photo courtesy of Penobscot Marine Museum*

Inside the *Foster D.*　　*Photo courtesy of Jameson family collection*

According to Pat Jameson Havener and Margaret Wotton Gagnon, the Jameson & Wotton Company wharf became a hub of the community. Marion Little Waters, lifelong summer resident, wrote, "My parents arrived at the wharf with the steamboat from Boston when they honeymooned at the family cottage in 1921." Manufactured goods arrived by boat, as opposed to over poor roads. The wharf was the gateway to the rest of the world.

At the beginning of the 20th century the Jameson & Wotton wharf was as long, but not as wide, as the current wharf. A tinted postcard dated 1913 shows the steamboat at the end of the wharf, the small ticket booth, a large storage building for dry goods, the store, a Friendship sloop beached beside the wharf, and at the land end a residence with four horse-drawn buggies waiting for passengers. The store, which sold dry goods, fishing gear, as well as some food products, especially penny candy, was a principal market for those who lived on the islands. When Sherm Jameson was collecting lobsters from the families on the islands in his lobster smack, the *Foster D.,* they would give him shopping lists for the store. When he next returned he would deliver their orders.

Sherm Jameson asked Walter H. Wotton (1864 – 1940) to become his partner in the wharf in 1897. Walter ran the store and kept the books while Sherm ran the waterfront, bought and sold lobsters and clams, and oversaw the steamboat trade. In 1900 Walter married Mary Etta, and they moved into their new house with fine gingerbread decoration at the crest of Harbor Road hill, then overlooking the harbor and the wharf. Coincidentally, Sherm Jameson and Mima lived directly across Harbor Road. Walter was described thus in his obituary: "He held the place of one of the most prosperous and industrious business men in the town, with a genial disposition and a pleasant smile for everyone." Today his granddaughter, Margaret Wotton Gagnon, the archivist for the Wotton family, lives in his house and has restored it to much as it was when Walter and Mary lived in it.

According to the historical journal kept by William Jameson, Sherm's grandson, "...in 1901 Gramp had the *Foster D.* (named for William's father) built on a model he had made himself. It was one of the first power boats in Friendship and had the lines of a sloop with a sharp clipper bow and rounded overhanging stern. There was a well amidships with holes bored thru the bottom so the water would circulate for the lobsters transported there." An article in the *Maine Coast Fisherman* (August 1948) featured Capt. Sherman Jameson and his use of lobster gauges. Also pictured were Sherm and his grandson William on the *Foster D.,* weighing lobsters collected from Teel's Island. This unique craft worked for over 45 years as a lobster smack in Muscongus Bay. To many Friendship residents of today, the memory of the *Foster D.,* anchored off the end of the wharf, was a heartwarming sight.

The economies of the outside world tended to dictate the fate of life in this coastal community. The consequences of WWI limited coastal traffic. The two hotels closed; my grandfather benefited by buying one of the Argyle Inn buildings in 1918, which is now our summer cottage, still with the room numbers on the upstairs doors. Nevertheless,

Friendship remained a quiet coastal town. Shell fishing for clams and lobsters, boat building, handlining for cod, etc., were the commercial industries of the town. The steamboat ran to points known and unknown until it ceased in the late 1920s. In 1928 Jameson and Wotton closed, and the wharf was sold to Charlie and Ida Stenger.

In a recent letter from Tom Stenger, Charlie and Ida's son, he tells that his parents opened the Lobster Pot restaurant in 1930 at the end of the wharf. The brochure states: "Home Cooked Food **** Lobsters and Clams – Served in all ways. Also Fish and Scallops. Pavilion for Picnics." There were 8 to 10 tables with generous windows that looked upon the activities of the harbor. Many members of the Friendship community fondly remember tasty shore dinners followed by blueberry pies. It remained open until 1956, when the wharf was sold to Bernard Brow, except for WWII when it was closed while Charlie worked at Bath Iron Works and Ida was a registered nurse. Charlie led the town Civil Defense corps and built an enemy plane spotter booth at the end of the dock. Men and women of the community stood duty 24 hours a day, but never saw an enemy plane.

Bob Stenger, Tom's brother, tells of the lobster smack *Mayflower,* owned by Chris Burns in the 1950s that was tied up at the end of the wharf, that transported lobsters from Friendship to Portland. Tom tells of a previous smack, *Conqueror,* that caught fire one night and had to be towed across the harbor and beached on the bar off the north point of Friendship Long Island, the remains of which could be seen for decades. Today the original wharf is the Friendship Lobster Co-op, busy every day buying and shipping lobsters to the markets of the world.

Tom Stenger closes with, "A lot of time us kids would gather on the wharf, in the evening, go fishing, swimming or what ever," and that about sums it up. The Jameson & Wotton/Stenger wharf, 1897 to 1956: so many memories, so many stories linked to the ocean gateway of the community of Friendship.

The *Foster D.* at Stenger Wharf   *Photo by Chub Patch courtesy of the Friendship Library*

21 *The Burt Murphy House* By Nancy Bellhouse May

An 1899 account indicates that Burt Murphy had just built himself a "commodious" house on Davis Point.[1] This might have been an understatement. The white clapboard house with a wrap-around porch was indeed large, and as it and the attached barn were sited just up the hill from his wharf and just down that hill from the shingled carriage houses that faced each other across his gravel drive, the whole property must have looked imposing.

Inside, the house's high-ceilinged rooms were trimmed with wide moldings that included corner rosettes and deep baseboards. The windows—even the two large windows whose lower sashes were constructed without muntins—were made of hand-blown glass, the floors were hardwood, the stairway banister had turned spindles and substantial newel posts, and the living-room fireplace had an ornate surround extending almost to the ceiling. Each of the three bedrooms included a large closet, and each was furnished with at least one oak washstand, three of which are still in the house today.

By the standards of the 1890s, the house had an up-to-date heating system. The living room was heated by the fireplace, the dining room and the front bedroom by stoves connected to the chimney flue, the kitchen by the six-burner cast-iron cookstove, and the remaining two bedrooms by ceiling vents in the dining room and kitchen. Also, everyone went up to bed with warm covers, because the house included a blanket closet built into a wall that backed up to the chimney.

The house's stone-and-mortar cellar was

Stone walls at Frances Creamer Richardson's home, built by Burt Murphy for Lorenzo Creamer.

Photo by Patricia Winchenbach

served by two stairways, one opening off the kitchen and another under the bulkhead door in the side yard. The barn, outfitted with a hayloft, deep bins for feed storage, and a full stone-and-mortar cellar of its own (in which Mr. Murphy quartered his mules), was connected to the house by a shed opening off the kitchen. Like the cellars, the foundations of both buildings were of stone and mortar, and the mortar on the house's foundation walls was tinted a deep red.

Mr. Murphy probably built the cellars and foundation walls himself, as he was an expert mason. The stone walls on the grounds of the Davis Point cottage then known as The Spruces[2] were Mr. Murphy's, as were those on the grounds of the summer home then owned by Lorenzo Creamer of Newton, Massachusetts, on School Street uptown.[3]

Because his was the first house built on the harbor side of Davis Point, Mr. Murphy had from his porch an unobstructed view down to his wharf and across to Friendship Long Island, and he could see up to the head of the harbor and out the mouth of the harbor to Muscongus Bay. Those views made the property desirable to later purchasers, but Burt Murphy was probably more interested in business than in scenic beauty; he wanted to see the shipments of coal, lumber, and wood arriving at and leaving from his wharf. (Despite more than 100 years of construction and tree growth in the area, it is still possible to see down the wharf and across the harbor from both the porch and the living room of the Murphy house.)

The Murphy property was eventually split in a sale; the land and wharf on the harbor side of the road were separated from the lot on which the house, barn, and carriage houses were located. The house and its lot went first to Albert Morton and Lew Wallace and then to Philip and Meredith Jarvis, about whom little is now known. Alma Black, who has lived nearby in the Winchenbaugh house since 1929, remembers only that the Jarvis family, whose winter home was in Somers, Connecticut, included a daughter named Ann, and that they stacked their canned goods on the floor of the Murphy house's sunny kitchen.[4] The single identifiable Jarvis souvenir that remains in the house is a wooden hanger apparently dating from Mr. Jarvis's col-

The Burt Murphy house in winter 2007.

Photo by Victor Motyka

lege years, for it is inscribed "Jarvis—TKE House."

For whatever reason, the Murphy house didn't suit the Jarvises, and they sold it in 1950 to Alan Bellhouse of Marblehead, Massachusetts, whose family had emigrated from England to the United States when he was a boy. Surprisingly enough, Alan Bellhouse had a connection to Burt Murphy. He and his mother Florence had spent every summer from 1920 through 1928 at The Spruces as guests of the Rauskolb family, and he remembered his mother laying the first stone for one of its Murphy-built walls.[5]

A graduate of the Massachusetts Nautical School (now the Massachusetts Maritime Academy), Alan Bellhouse was a shipmaster whose work kept him abroad for months at a time. Florence, who had been widowed in the 1920s, lived alone in the house for much of the year. She was a gardener of some note. The pine trees that surround the house and barn, the hedge of boxwood and forsythia that runs perpendicular to the barn, the lilac bushes on both sides of the driveway, the floribunda hedges that separate the lawns from the road, and the remnants of the large flower gardens between the house and the driveway are the lasting evidence of the hours she devoted to the grounds. She was also known for the fine quality of her knitting, and the surviving examples of her work (a sweater and two treasured Christmas stockings) indicate that her reputation was well deserved.

In Marblehead, Captain Bellhouse had turned his navigational charts to good use as he replaced them, papering the foyer of his house with a selection of outdated charts showing ports and harbors around the world. He continued this tradition in the Murphy house, using his outdated charts to paper the walls and ceiling of the shed. Roof leaks and plumbing emergencies (most spectacular among them the geyser that spouted from a burst pipe one winter day in the 1960s) required their periodic replacement, and those currently on display are the last of the charts that he brought home when he retired. They include a great circle chart of the world and charts showing ports in places like Germany, the United Arab Emirates, and Puerto Rico; several bear handwritten notations indicating the preferred headings for each approach.

After Alan Bellhouse married Dorothy Lyons in 1953, settled in New York City, and started a family, the house was slowly modernized, beginning with the installation of baseboard heat in the mid-1950s. The Bellhouses continued to visit the Murphy house in the summers, and once they moved to the house in the early fall of 1962, the updating continued at a faster pace. Among those projects were a series of kitchen remodels that included the removal of the huge woodstove; the covering of the wood floors throughout the house with linoleum and carpet; and the conversion of the shed into a laundry room. The most dramatic change in the house occurred earlier, however, when the side portion of the porch was removed in the early 1950s and replaced with a small first-floor bedroom for Florence, who was by then suffering from arthritis. This was perhaps the most curious change in the house, for the only inside entry to the new room was through a tiny downstairs bath constructed at the same time. (An upstairs bathroom had been added to the house sometime before 1950, in space cannibalized from a bedroom closet and one end of the upstairs hall.) This downstairs bedroom was converted to a den in the

mid-1960s, and a new doorway was then cut from the den through to the hall.

The only significant change elsewhere on the property was the removal of one of the carriage houses in the early 1960s. It was moved at that time to a spot near the corner of Route 220 and the Finntown Road, where it appears still to be in use today.

Visitors to the Murphy house often notice that it reflects Alan Bellhouse's long career as a shipmaster. In addition to the charts in the shed, the moldings above the doors into the kitchen and the den bear brass plates reading, respectively, "CREW" and "CAPTAIN'S OFFICE" that were taken from a decommissioned freight ship being dismantled for scrap. A shelf above the bay window in the dining room showcases a selection of china plates bearing the insignia of passenger lines that have long since disappeared, and displayed around the house are exotic shells and bits of coral, a hand-carved tiki, and photos and paintings with maritime themes.

Although Captain Bellhouse was at sea during the era in which American shipping dominated world commerce, his career, like that of most men of his generation, was interrupted by World War II. Commissioned an officer in the Naval Reserve upon graduating from MNS, he was called to active duty in 1940, serving first on a series of escort ships accompanying the merchant vessels that carried lend-lease equipment to England. He spent most of the war in the Pacific, however, serving his longest stint as the executive officer on an aircraft carrier supporting a squadron of Marine fighter planes. He returned to commercial shipping after the war, retiring as captain of the container ship *SeaTrain TransColumbia* in 1974.

After the deaths of Alan and Dorothy Bellhouse, the Murphy house passed to their daughters, making their grandson the fourth generation of the Bellhouse family to have a connection to the Murphy house, to Davis Point, and to Friendship.

"Dinner bell" on the porch of the house that Captain Bellhouse brought home from one of his journeys. His wife, Dorothy, rang it to call him home when he was working on his sailboat in the harbor.   *Photo by Polly Jones*

The Burt Murphy wharf in the 1950s.   *Photo courtesy of the Friendship Library, Chubb Patch collection*

22 *The General Ellis Spear Cottage* By Julie Spear Pugh

General Ellis Spear (1834-1917) served as second in command to Joshua Chamberlain of the 20th Maine Regiment in the Civil War, in battles including Fredericksburg, Chancellorsville, Rappahannock Station, The Wilderness, Petersburg, and Little Round Top (Gettysburg).[1] Ellis Spear had graduated from Bowdoin College in 1858 and entered the National Army in August 1862 as a Captain of the 20th Maine Volunteer Infantry. During the Civil War, he rose through the ranks rapidly. In September 1864, Spear was brevetted Lieutenant Colonel of Volunteers for "gallant and distinguished services at the Battle of Peebles farm, Virginia." On Sunday, April 9, 1865, Spear was brevetted Brigadier General. On that same day, General Spear was a witness to General Robert E. Lee's surrender of the Confederate Army of Northern Virginia to General Ulysses S. Grant in the village of Appomattox Court House.

The General Ellis Spear Cottage in fall 2006.

Girl on Swing by Arthur Spear (painted in Friendship).   *Photo by Jack Pugh*

the Warren farm). Arthur and his wife, Grace, summered here until their deaths, when their daughter Pauline Spear Chapin and her family inherited the property. Spear family descendents summering here are now in the sixth generation.

A popular Impressionist artist from Boston, Arthur built his 1910 studio (now Dunipace) on the eastern boundary of the property. He painted many of his mermaid and fish scenes there. His children and friends were among his models. He also carved and gilded his picture frames and hooked rugs with the fish and fauna motifs. Many of his artist friends

General Ellis Spear.   *Photo courtesy of the Maine State Archives*

vacationed at the cottage, where fishing, feasting, as well as painting, were popular pastimes. On several foggy weekends when they were housebound, Arthur Crisp, Harry Hoffman, Let Thompson, and other artists contributed their talents to illustrating the four door panels and the mantelpiece in the living room.

In the cottage are many of Arthur's pastels and old photos of the house and property as well as a framed 1913 tax bill for $15.40!

At the conclusion of the war, Spear became an examiner for the United States Patent Office. In 1874 he was promoted to Assistant Commissioner of Patents. In January 1877, President Grant appointed Spear Commissioner of Patents of the United States. He resigned in November 1878, when he began a practice as an attorney and solicitor in patent cases. He made his home in Washington, D.C., where he died on April 3, 1917. He is buried in Section 2 of Arlington National Cemetery with his second wife, Sarah, who also died in 1917.[2]

Returning from the War, General Ellis Spear purchased the south-western tip of Davis Point from his Davis relatives. The spectacular view from this promontory to the southwest is of Ram, Sand, and Long islands plus distant islands in Muscongus Bay. To the east is the anchorage and fishing harbor of Friendship. The flat rocks in front of the cottage, heated by the day's sun, are perfect for picnicking and viewing the sunsets behind Ram and Sand islands. He used the Friendship property for camping and fishing until 1900 when he built Sea Ledge, the first seasonal cottage on Davis Point. Ellis's brother Jason Spear helped with the carpentry for the new home and used lumber from the family farm on Route 1 in Warren.[3]

Ellis's first wife, Susie Wilde, died in 1873. In 1875 he married Sarah Prince Keene, whose husband, Samuel J. Keene (a close friend of Ellis's) died in Ellis's arms during the war. The Keene family subsequently built the cottage next door to the west (now Waters). Spear relatives later owned the 1906 cottage on the eastern border (now gh). Upon General Ellis's death, Sea Ledge was left to his son hur Prince Spear, Sr. (Arthur's brother Edwin Ellis (Ned) inherited

Foolish Fish by Arthur Spear, painted on the living room fireplace.   *Photo by Jack Pugh*

22 *The General Ellis Spear Cottage* *By Julie Spear Pugh*

General Ellis Spear (1834-1917) served as second in command to Joshua Chamberlain of the 20th Maine Regiment in the Civil War, in battles including Fredericksburg, Chancellorsville, Rappahannock Station, The Wilderness, Petersburg, and Little Round Top (Gettysburg).[1] Ellis Spear had graduated from Bowdoin College in 1858 and entered the National Army in August 1862 as a Captain of the 20th Maine Volunteer Infantry. During the Civil War,

he rose through the ranks rapidly. In September 1864, Spear was brevetted Lieutenant Colonel of Volunteers for "gallant and distinguished services at the Battle of Peebles farm, Virginia." On Sunday, April 9, 1865, Spear was brevetted Brigadier General. On that same day, General Spear was a witness to General Robert E. Lee's surrender of the Confederate Army of Northern Virginia to General Ulysses S. Grant in the village of Appomattox Court House.

The General Ellis Spear Cottage in fall 2006.

Photo by Polly Jones

Girl on Swing by Arthur Spear (painted in Friendship).   *Photo by Jack Pugh*

General Ellis Spear.   *Photo courtesy of the Maine State Archives*

the Warren farm). Arthur and his wife, Grace, summered here until their deaths, when their daughter Pauline Spear Chapin and her family inherited the property. Spear family descendents summering here are now in the sixth generation.

A popular Impressionist artist from Boston, Arthur built his 1910 studio (now Dunipace) on the eastern boundary of the property. He painted many of his mermaid and fish scenes there. His children and friends were among his models. He also carved and gilded his picture frames and hooked rugs with the fish and fauna motifs. Many of his artist friends vacationed at the cottage, where fishing, feasting, as well as painting, were popular pastimes. On several foggy weekends when they were housebound, Arthur Crisp, Harry Hoffman, Let Thompson, and other artists contributed their talents to illustrating the four door panels and the mantelpiece in the living room.

In the cottage are many of Arthur's pastels and old photos of the house and property as well as a framed 1913 tax bill for $15.40!

At the conclusion of the war, Spear became an examiner for the United States Patent Office. In 1874 he was promoted to Assistant Commissioner of Patents. In January 1877, President Grant appointed Spear Commissioner of Patents of the United States. He resigned in November 1878, when he began a practice as an attorney and solicitor in patent cases. He made his home in Washington, D.C., where he died on April 3, 1917. He is buried in Section 2 of Arlington National Cemetery with his second wife, Sarah, who also died in 1917.[2]

Returning from the War, General Ellis Spear purchased the south-western tip of Davis Point from his Davis relatives. The spectacular view from this promontory to the southwest is of Ram, Sand, and Long islands plus distant islands in Muscongus Bay. To the east is the anchorage and fishing harbor of Friendship. The flat rocks in front of the cottage, heated by the day's sun, are perfect for picnicking and viewing the sunsets behind Ram and Sand islands. He used the Friendship property for camping and fishing until 1900 when he built Sea Ledge, the first seasonal cottage on Davis Point. Ellis's brother Jason Spear helped with the carpentry for the new home and used lumber from the family farm on Route 1 in Warren.[3]

Ellis's first wife, Susie Wilde, died in 1873. In 1875 he married Sarah Prince Keene, whose husband, Samuel J. Keene (a close friend of Ellis's) died in Ellis's arms during the war. The Keene family subsequently built the cottage next door to the west (now Waters). Spear relatives later owned the 1906 cottage on the eastern border (now Pugh). Upon General Ellis's death, Sea Ledge was left to his son Arthur Prince Spear, Sr. (Arthur's brother Edwin Ellis (Ned) inherited

Foolish Fish by Arthur Spear, painted on the living room fireplace. *Photo by Jack Pugh*

Town of *Friendship* Maine

M. Ellis & Arthur Spear

Your State, County and Town Tax for the year 1913 is as follows:

Poll, $
Real Estate, 1540
Personal Estate,
Total Tax, $ 15 40

Received Payment, *Aug 3* 191

E.A. Burns Collector.

Rate of Taxation, $ 22 per $1,000.

Arthur and Ellis Spears' tax bill from 1913.

Photo by Jack Pugh

Sarah Prince Keene Spear and General Ellis Spear.

From the collection of Julie Spear Pugh

Experience Friendship

Visit the Friendship Library and search
their valuable cache of historic records.

Relax, leaving all cares behind,
as you vacation in Friendship.

Enjoy a mug up with a friend
as the sun rises in the east.

In the evening go rowing in the harbor,
delighting in the glow of the fluorescence
with each dip of the oars.

Hold a barbecue on your lawn
with your family, friends and neighbors.

Look forward to corn on the cob
slathered with real butter.

Marguerite C. Sylvester

View of Ram Island and Sand Island from Davis Point.

Photo by Celia Lash Briggs

23 *The Wilbur Morse House* By Priscilla Wilder Ambrose

Perched on the side of the hill overlooking Friendship Harbor, this eye-catching house was built by Wilbur Morse in 1900. Prominent in all the old postcards taken at the beginning of the 20th century, it is now almost entirely obscured by the massive maples grown up around it.

Between the years 1893 and 1929, Wilbur Morse built almost 150 boats.[1] They were of various types and sizes but the majority of them were Friendship sloops that put our town of Friendship on the map and in the hearts and minds of seagoin' folk around the world.

Morse was born on Hungry Island in 1853, later moving to Bremen Long Island. Before boat building became his career on the mainland, he was a fisherman trying to cope with the demise of the big schooners as the main way of getting to the fishing banks. He and his fishing friends envisioned a smaller, more responsive craft that could be managed by a single individual, rather than being dependent on multiple masts and many hands.

The Morse brothers, other Morse relatives, as well as the vast population of fishing people in the community, put their heads together and designed a small sailing vessel. Typically, the men of those times desiring this type of boat would build a sloop over the winter months, use it during the fishing season, sell it, and build another over the next winter. Wilbur Morse's boat building history came

The Wilbur Morse home in Fall 2006.

Photo by Polly Jones

about in this manner. Before long he realized he could do better at boat building than at fishing. He built a shop for this purpose, and soon his future became secure. The first Friendship sloop from the shop was built, the price was right, and the orders kept coming.[2]

The early boatyard in Lawry and the one later built at the shore in Friendship harbor, in front of the house we are featuring in this article, were abuzz with activity. Morse was certainly an excellent craftsman, but his particular genius was in being a shrewd businessman to the point that he could be called the Henry Ford of Friendship sloops. He developed an assembly line approach for sloop building, a revolutionary concept. Morse and his crew of about twelve skilled workers launched an average of two boats a month, with sometimes five boats being built at once. Modern thinking resulted in a genera-

tor for power tools, and lights to ensure continued labor during short winter days.[3]

Through the decades published accounts have differed as to the actual history of the Friendship sloop. Wilbur Morse was without question the most well-known builder. He developed is own model and stayed true to this design with the 95 sloops built in his boatyard. Of the other hundreds built in this area, the design changed somewhat with every sloop, thus creating the variations in the boats then and continuing with the differences today. The sloops cost $450 complete, with the wives of the builders sewing the sails. In the 1920s the sloops were outfitted with the new gasoline engine and stayed in service while they continued to be seaworthy.[4]

Often with boat builders it was natural that they turn their skills to building their own homes. Such was the case with Wilbur Morse, who built his handsome house in 1900 overlooking Friendship harbor. The lumber for the house and boatyard came via schooner from Bangor. The house cost $1200 to build.[4] Through the years much of the early, abundant gingerbread was removed when the need to paint it became too much of a burden. Perhaps that was a good and practical decision because there is still much gingerbread present to please the eye. The boat shop, built directly at the water below the house in 1900 (and

Postcard of the Wilbur Morse boatyard.   *From the collection of Robert S. Lash, Jr.*

even more prominent in the old photos than the house), was torn down because of rot in the 1970s.[5] The cellar hole and some cement foundations are still evident.

Generations after the decline of the Friendship sloop as an important working boat, it experienced resurgence due to the appreciative eye of recreational sailors.

Detail of original cornice.   *Photo by Polly Jones*

Wilbur Morse in the foreground, Steamer *Brandon*.   *From the collection of Robert S. Lash, Jr.*

Boat on ways at Morse's Boat Shop in Friendship.   *From the collection of Robert S. Lash, Jr.*

It cost $150.00, which covered the cost of construction as well as "payment for land damages."[5] The following year (1873), Edward Thomas Jr. built his farmhouse and attached barn. His home was often referred to as "the big house" at the harbor.

In 1865 Edward Thomas Jr. (1843-1909) married Amanda Morse (1848-1913). Amanda was originally from Bremen Long Island. After marriage the couple lived on Friendship Long Island, not far from his parents, Edward Thomas Sr. and Mary Geyer Thomas. They lived near Minister's Gut. Edward Jr. and Amanda raised two daughters, Mamie (1866-1928) and Albertine (1870-1930), on Friendship Long Island before moving into the new, big house on the hillside. Both Amanda and Edward lived and died in their new home above the harbor.

In 1889 a most interesting set of weddings took place. In January, sister Mamie married Fessenden Wincapaw (1860-1952). In December of the same year, her sister, Albertine, married Elbridge A. Wincapaw (1867-1946). Yes, the two Thomas sisters married Wincapaw brothers. Not only that, they lived side by side on the same hillside. Albertine and Elbridge came to live in the big farmhouse, after the death of Albertine's mother, in 1913. Eventually, sister Mamie and Fessenden moved into a smaller house, next door, which was built in 1893.

Elbridge and Fessenden were but two of eight children born to Frederick and Lydia (Orne) Wincapaw. As an adult, Elbridge was a dedicated community leader, serving as selectman on several occasions. He was a mariner and ship owner. His 26' sloop, the *Lillian A.*, named after his niece, was built at the Morse boat shop in 1894.[6] He owned property on Friendship Long Island. Income was also derived from raising chickens and selling eggs. He died in 1946 at the age of 79. His brother, Fessenden, administered his estate. It was sold to Virginia E. Appel for $10,000 in 1947.[7] How property values have changed!

Virginia Appel married Edward Waldron. She and her husband and her

Edward Thomas Jr. house in the 1970s   *Photo by Bill Olsen*

sons, Ron and Jon, lived in the house for 15 years. Edward Waldron was retired from American Export Lines. Their nautical interests are evident in details throughout the house: exterior marine lights, ship-like ceiling beams, and wide views of Friendship harbor from the renovated living space that was once the attached barn and calf shed. Mellowed pine paneling creates a seaside cottage-like atmosphere in several rooms.

From 1960 to 1963 E. Merritt Post owned the property and was responsible for its subdivision. Jed Divine, photographer, and Friendship Long Island property owner, writes, "Merritt Post owned, operated, and to a large extent built the lobster pound on Little Morse Island, which he later sold to Coastal Fisheries. An eccentric, energetic adventurer from outside New York, Merritt was entertaining, charming, and thorny. He flew his own seaplane, with his dog, Drift, as copilot."[8]

Leopold and Evelyn Blum resided here from 1963 to 1974, after which William and Maude (Joan) Olsen came to Friendship from New Jersey. Maude, an accomplished artist and teacher, still exhibits her work throughout the midcoast area. Together with Bill, a professional

Aerial photo showing the Edward Thomas Jr. house in 1935.

Photo courtesy of Dorothy Burns Snowdeal

Aerial photo of Edward Thomas Jr. house and surrounding neighborhood, taken from Herb Micue's power-chute in fall 2002.

Photo by Chip Jahnke

photographer, they now live in South Bristol, Maine. They lived in Friendship from 1974 to 1986. In the Olsens' personal photo album was a treasure – an aerial view photo of our property with this inscription:

> To: Uncle E. Wincapaw
> From: W. H. Wincapaw
> 11/26/35

Bill Olsen still had the negative, enlarged it, and gave us the photo for this publication. Our neighborhood can be seen, with many historic homes and buildings still standing today.

Elbridge Wincapaw's aviator nephew is the legendary Rockland-based seaplane pilot and native Friendship son, Capt. William (Bill) Wincapaw, the original Flying Santa. From 1929 until his death in 1947, Capt. Bill Wincapaw dropped Christmas packages to U.S. Coast Guard lighthouse families as a gesture of thanks and appreciation for their life-saving assistance as he perilously navigated his small plane up and down the Maine coast. His son, Bill Jr., joined him on many flights, as did marine author and historian Edward Rowe Snow. On October 14, 2006, Capt. Bill Wincapaw was honored at a memorial plaque ceremony at the Maine Lighthouse Museum in Rockland.

A book for young readers, *The Flying Santa*,[9] by Joe and Paula McHugh, describes young William's childhood in Friendship. His young aviator skills are exemplified by his daring flight under New York City's Brooklyn Bridge. Bill Olsen and I have childhood connections to Brooklyn, and now our families are proud to have a Flying Santa connection as well.

Bill Olsen tells a wonderful story of another connection to the Wincapaws. In 1976 Bill sought to own a boat for tuna fishing. In Humarock, Massachusetts, he found a vessel built for swordfishing that suited his needs. Upon closer inspection he found the following

Bill Wincapaw, the Flying Santa, in his youth. *Photo courtesy Jameson family collection*

inscription in the hold: "1938 – F. Wincapaw, Friendship, Maine." Bill purchased the boat, named her "Maude," and moored her in Friendship, below Fessenden's former home. Sadly, Bill never did catch a tuna![10]

Ever since Dr. William Stroud and Rev. Steven Law established Harbor Hill B & B (ownership 1986-1989), the exterior doors of the house have been painted that welcoming red color. When Chip and I purchased our home from Dennis Churchman (ownership 1989-1992), we decided to retain the Harbor Hill name and have greeted visitors, guests, friends, and family to Friendship since 1992. Skyler, and Tucker before him, announces everyone's arrival with enthusiastic barks!

Early patterns of settlement in Friendship reflect many varied origins. Whether folks in Friendship have long-established roots or have come in more recent times, this richness in backgrounds continues to be evident: Chip was born in Hartford, Connecticut, and I, across the Atlantic, in Riga, Latvia. Living in the historic Edward Thomas Jr./Elbridge Wincapaw house has given us a strong link to Friendship's history. It has also connected us to adopted roots that we value and celebrate in 2007 and will continue to celebrate in the years to come.

Watercolor from Edward Thomas Jr. house showing the general outline of Harbor Hill (calf shed, barn, house), painted by Maude Olsen when she lived here. *Courtesy of Maude Olsen*

"A Warm Welcome," watercolor of the open front door of the Edward Thomas Jr. house, painted by Katharina Keoughan in 1998. *Courtesy of Liga V. and Chip Jahnke*

Living room of the Thomas farm, early 1900s.   *From the collection of Robert S. Lash, Jr.*

Postcard of the Thomas farm, circa 1900.   *From the collection of Robert S. Lash, Jr.*

View of houses during the Camp Wehinahpay years.   *From the collection of Robert S. Lash, Jr.*

The remaining Thomas barn, as it stands today.   *Photo by Celia Lash Briggs*

Blackfish Day

The cove at the head of the harbor has been called by at least four names. Some know it as Johnston Cove from the Johnston House Inn that was there in the late 19th century. In the early 20th century it was called Clark Ledge Cove. Others remember it by an earlier name, Shipyard Cove, due to a boat yard operated by Nelson Thompson and Zenas Cook. Perhaps the most interesting name of all is Blackfish Cove, owing to the events of a stormy December morning in 1874.

As the morning snowstorm abated, the fishermen of Friendship were amazed to see the harbor teeming with blackfish, also known as pilot whales. Soon the men rowed to the mouth of the harbor, formed a line, and began driving the whales into the cove. The fish were stranded in the shoal water, and the fishermen were able to harvest 150 barrels of oil and enough blubber to cover the decks of three large schooners. Dodd and Company of Gloucester, Massachusetts, paid 2 cents a pound for the blubber, and the heads netted $1.25 to $1.50 each. Twelve hundred dollars worth of oil was rendered. One hundred eighty-one fish were taken, the largest weighing almost two tons at 19 feet long. The oldest fisherman could not remember ever seeing a blackfish inside of George's Island before.

V Bradford Point

Photo by Elaine Lang Cornett

26 *Captain Albert Gallatin Cook House* By Eleanor Cook Lang

Eleanor Cook Lang.   *Photo courtesy Elaine Lang Cornett*

As you crest the first hill heading toward the end of Bradford Point, you pass the long stretch of a white New England farmhouse. This is the Captain Cook family home, built by Albert and Mary Jane Cook in 1860. Local master carpenter David Bessey worked with Albert to design and build the house. Another Cook brother, Henry, was Bessey's assistant.

The land for the house came from an uncle, Francis Cook, and was adjacent to land owned by Bradford Cook, Albert's father. The original building consisted of the house, an ell, and an attached barn. After about ten years Mary Jane decided she wanted a larger kitchen and a dining room, so the barn was converted into a kitchen, a washroom and a shed with a workshop above it. The former kitchen became a dining room, and a separate barn was built behind the house. To this day, an old bell formerly worn by one of the cows that lived in that barn hangs from the ceiling of the dining room. It is used now as a dinner bell.

Cook house circa 1860.   *From the collection of Eleanor Cook Lang*

The house was quite modern for its time. A privy was attached to the shed. No going outside in the cold weather! To supplement the dug well out behind the house, a brick cistern was built under the kitchen to catch rainwater from the roof. The kitchen sink had a pump to dispense the rainwater. There was a woodhouse built onto the end of the shed. There were no fireplaces in the house, only wood or coal stoves. This was considered a fine house with an efficient heating system, running water and indoor "plumbing."

Although they were not farmers, Albert and Mary Jane had a small farm to support their own needs, as did most people in the area. They had cows, a pig, chickens, an orchard and a vegetable garden. A wooded area down near the water on the Back River was their source for firewood. Parts of the stone wall that lined the route to the cow pasture can still be found winding through the trees behind the house.

Albert Cook was captain of a series of three-masted cargo schooners. The last and largest of these was the *Mary J. Cook,* named for his wife. The ship was built in Waldoboro, which was at the time the location of a thriving shipbuilding trade. Capt. Cook's home port was New York City, and he sailed up and down the East Coast, the Gulf Coast, in the Caribbean and sometimes to South America.

Born in 1829, he was named for the respected statesman and prominent financier Albert Gallatin. He started going to sea at the age of fourteen as a cabinboy for his uncle, James Cook. By the age 25 he was his uncle's first mate. In 1857 he received his first ship as a wedding present from Squire Zenas Cook, Mary Jane's uncle. He retired from the sea at age 54, saddened by the death of his oldest son, Winfred, who had been his first mate. A further loss was the man who replaced Win as first mate. During a terrible hurricane off Cape Hatteras, the

main boom broke and hit him in the chest, crushing him. The schooner survived, but the mate did not.

In 1921, when Albert and Mary Jane died within two months of each other, the house and land passed to Albert's youngest son, Raymond (my father). Raymond was a school principal in Massachusetts and had always spent his summers helping his father with the upkeep of the place. He made very few changes but did add electricity when it came to Bradford Point in 1945. His hobby was gardening and he devoted his retirement to beautifying the grounds. The orchard he planted and the flower gardens are now

Mary Jane Cook's coffeepot filled with sea lavender adorns a buttery corner shelf. *Photo by Elaine Lang Cornett*

mostly gone, but many trees and bushes remain. His pride and joy was a magnificent Japanese walnut tree, whose "children" now grace the yards of many relatives and friends.

In 1951 the house passed to me on the death of my father. As soon as I could afford it, I put in contemporary plumbing (a drilled well, septic tank, bathroom and laundry facilities), although my mother used a washstand in her upstairs bedroom as long as she lived. When we brought in a crew to drill the well, I told them to start with the spot my father had always

Watercolor by Marion Powers Kirkpatrick, who used a daguerreotype of eighteen-year-old Mary Jane Geyer to create the painting. *Photo by Elaine Lang Cornett*

Mary J. Cook painted by Edith Stevens in 1970. *Photo by Elaine Lang Cornett*

pointed to when he talked about finding good water for a well someday. As it turned out, his instincts were right, just as they usually were about this home that he loved so much. The drill machine struck an abundant supply of good water at 60 feet, exactly where he said it would be.

Much later, we also replaced the old woodshed and privy with a garage. A dormer has been added to the "open chamber" where, as boys, my father and his brothers used to sleep dormitory style. With more light and air, it will again serve as a pleasant haven and playroom for present and future generations of children and, possibly, once more as a dormitory if we outgrow our six bedrooms. Except for these few modifications, the interior and exterior of the house look much as they did over 100 years ago.

The Captain Albert Gallatin Cook house today.

Photo by Elaine Lang Cornett

27 *Miss Margaret's House* By Eleanor Cook Lang

This classic cape with a magnificent view of the harbor is the oldest house still standing on Bradford Point. It was built before 1800 (probably about 1795) by one of the original Cook brothers – most likely James, since his wife, Elsie, is listed as owner in 1803. It was built on the foundations of an older house that had burned down. The ell and attached barn would have been added later. On a clear day one can see all the way out to Monhegan from the back windows.

James Cook (1749-1798) was probably lost at sea. His death left his wife to raise eight young children alone. Elsie is listed in town records as having a school in this house in the winter of 1807. Her son, Cornelius, is the one who is recorded in family history as hearing guns and seeing puffs of smoke off Monhegan in September of 1813. This was during the War of 1812, and it was known that British and American naval forces were in the area. He grabbed a spyglass and ran to the top of the High Hill on Bradford Point to watch the famous battle between the *Boxer* and the *Enterprise*. He was able to report with great joy the American victory, since when the battle was over both ships turned and "sailed to the westward" toward Portland. Francis Cook, another son, owned the house in the 1850s. Elsie Cook died in 1851.

William Newbert and his family lived here for a time in the 1870s and 1880s. William was elected town treasurer in 1880. His wife, "Aunt

Photo postcard of Paul and Margaret Simmons sent to Lena Cushman (Mrs. Newell Cushman) postmarked 8/15/1913. *From the collection of Eva Jane Simmons Demers*

Tin," was a good friend of my grandmother, Mary Jane Cook. My father, as a little boy, played with their daughter Flora Estelle, who later married John Dodge of Spruce Head.

In 1901, Samuel Simmons and his wife, Mary Cushman Simmons, bought the house from Morton Bessey. They had moved to Friendship from Cow Island with their four children in 1886. Sam was both a deep-sea and lobster fisherman, although after 1901 he concentrated on farming. He and his wife lived to very advanced ages – Mary dying at 94 and Sam at 95. They were married for 73 years.

Mary Cushman Simmons and Samuel Simmons.

From the collection of Eva Jane Simmons Demers

Paul, his mother, Lillian, Margaret and Myron Simmons

From the collection of Eva Jane Simmons Demers

Their youngest son, Owen, inherited the home in the early 1940s. He was a yachtsman who captained several yachts for wealthy summer visitors. Owen was also a lobster fisherman in his later years, as well as a boat builder. During World War II he and his son Paul supported the war effort by working at Snow's shipyard in Rockland, building wooden-hulled vessels for anti-submarine warfare. This was already considered a very specialized art.

Owen and his wife, Lillian Bramhall Simmons, had three children: Paul, Myron, and Margaret.

Miss Margaret Simmons, circa 1940.

From the collection of Eva Jane Simmons Demers

Margaret, a schoolteacher, helped pay for her education by cooking during the summer for Harry Thompson of *Moxie* fame at his place on Friendship Long Island. Fortunately for his guests, she was a wonderful cook, having learned from her mother, also well known for her culinary skills.

A most talented teacher, she gave up a good position and came back to Friendship to look after her mother in her final illness. Margaret then taught at the Village School in town for many years, much to the benefit of Friendship's children. She was one of

The ell of the Miss Margaret Simmons house as it stands today.

Photo by Elaine Lang Cornett

those who were responsible for the excellent library Friendship has today.

Her brothers, Paul and Myron, settled on Bradford Point and raised their families in houses just a few hundred yards from their childhood home.

Owen Simmons died in 1965, leaving the family home to Margaret. She had never married and had no children. On a teacher's pension, she found it difficult to keep the place up to her high stan-dards, saying that old houses need constant care. In 1989 she sold the house to Debbie Deal, the present owner. Debbie is an artist and landscape gardener who manages to grow an abundance of beautiful flowers in this rocky Maine soil. She has rebuilt the barn, which is now her studio and workshop, and partially restored the house to the way it was in the nineteenth century.

The back of the house, barn, and outbuilding from Debbie Deal's garden in 2006.

Photo by Elaine Lang Cornett

Frederick Young in his WWI uniform.   *Photo courtesy Friendship Museum*

F. Bradford Young in his grandfather's WWI uniform.   *Photo by Adolfo Chavez III*

cooking. He ran downstairs, happily saying "We're having bacon for breakfast, aren't we?" To which his grandmother said, " No, no bacon." When he said he was sure he had smelled bacon, Bertha simply smiled and said that people who slept in that particular room often smelled bacon in the morning. Along with special childhood memories Brad Young has as a reminder of his family's history, his grandfather's World War I uniform jacket. It is now a cherished memento for the current Young family.

Philippe Von Hemert.   *Photo by Elaine Lang Cornett*

Philippe Von Hemert, who bought the house in 1973, did necessary repairs, but he left the outside very much as it had always been, with one exception. The roof, which needed to be re-shingled, had for years been red. He changed it to a neutral grey, which he was later told caused old sailors some trouble, as they had always used it as a marker when coming into Friendship harbor. "Steer for the red roof"[3] was known up and down the coast as the landmark for Friendship.

The ell has been redone into a beautiful great room on the first floor, and two large bedrooms replaced the eight small ones on the second floor. Full advantage of the unparalleled view has been taken. Joshua Bradford chose wisely when he built his log cabin on this beautiful spot.

Bertha Young's Hard Soap Recipe

One can potash
One half cup of Borax
One half cup of ammonia
One quart cold water
Five pound of grease.

Pour water over potash. Let cool until lukewarm. Strain grease and have it just lukewarm. Pour grease slowly into lye.

Jennie Speed says she puts two tablespoons of kerosene in her soap, made the same as above.

Caution: Never pour water over a strong alkali, such as potash. The resulting chemical reaction can heat the water to steam instantly, causing an explosion of the corrosive mixture. Better to add water to the lye slowly.

Bertha Young's Toilet Soap Recipe

One can potash
One quart cold water
Twenty cents worth of glycerine
Two tablespoons of Borax
One cup of almond meal
Bergamont (bergamot)
Six pounds of grease

Put potash in cold water; add glycerine, borax, meal and oil, after it is dissolved and cool. Let the grease be strained and just melted, not hot.

Stir grease into mixture. Stir until it looks like cream. Pour into pan or corset boxes. Cut into squares before quite hard. Be sure and not put the meal in while the lye is hot as it cooks it.

Ocean Breeze Hotel, Friendship, Me.

From the collection of Robert S. Lash, Jr.

$\boxed{V}$ Martin Point

Scott and Wayne Delano clamming in Hatchet Cove, winter 2007.

29 The George Pottle House— The Home Away from the Sea By Patricia Winchenbach

"This summer I didn't get down to the village more than twice. They got water – sea water – down there. So long as I don't see any of that sea water, I'm as happy as a dog with two tails!"

Strange that anyone living in Friendship would feel that way about the ocean, but those were the sentiments of 65-year-old Willie Pottle when interviewed for *The Maine Coast Fisherman* in November 1957. "I build dories," he said, "but I haven't been to sea in one of them yet. I was born on a lighthouse island and spent the first eight years of my life surrounded by water. I had all the water I'll ever want to see!" It could be that his father, George Pottle, during his lifetime, came to feel exactly the same way.

George Pottle, born the seventh and last child of Daniel Pottle and his wife, Katherine, came from Searsport to live in Friendship in 1860 when he was just a 10-year-old lad. Phoebe, who also grew up in Searsport, and her husband, Joshua Davis, accepted the responsibility of raising George following his mother's untimely death. Years later, George married and spent 10 years living here on the mainland raising a family of three children. In 1883 he and his wife, Arvilla, moved off-shore to Harbor Island. The island lifestyle must have suited his family, because in 1888 George accepted a position as keeper of the Franklin Island Lighthouse, and there on the island, they made their home for the next 12 years. In the fourth year of George and Arvilla's island existence, 15 years after their third child had been born, William O. Pottle (Willie) came into this world—and of course he *was* surrounded by water! Earlier, children Ava, Oletha, and Alvin had been born.

It's interesting how stories get handed down and passed along, each teller perhaps tweaking the lines a bit to make the story more interesting.

Pottle house, circa 1920s.

Photo courtesy of Gordon and Pat Winchenbach

But sometimes, like in the game I remember from my childhood, *Secrets,* where the players form a circle and one person whispers something to the next person, and that person whispers it to the next, and so on, the stories get changed because a name or a word was misunderstood or altered in the retelling. This may be the case with the history of the George Pottle house. *Most likely,* after more than 15 years of island-living, George, and Arvilla too, had had all of the oceanfront experience they needed to last a lifetime and were looking forward to the end of their watery assignment. Town accounts have it that it was George who was determined to purchase a nice *inland* piece of land where he could raise some chickens, plant some crops, and perhaps open a small convenience store.

The perfect answer to George's desires presented itself in the timely offering of a house for sale by Herbert Parsons in 1897. "Mr. Parsons had built the house on the top of Martin Point Road in 1896 when he expected to marry Miss Edith Benner of South Waldoboro. However, they decided not to marry and he (Mr. Parsons) left the house unfinished."[1] Herbert agreed to sell the house and property, with the exception of a piece of land he set off for his sister, Millie Parsons, for a price of $1,050.00. That piece of land would eventually become the home of one of Friendship's well-known boat builders, Charles Morse.

When 1900 finally arrived, George, Arvilla, and now 8-year-old Willie moved to solid ground—inland—a full half mile from the ocean! Who wanted the sure footing and tillable soil beneath his feet more, Willie or George? Sometimes fathers and sons have trouble finding common

Young Willie Pottle.
Photo courtesy of Gordon and Pat Winchenbach

Willie Pottle with several of his dories. *Photo courtesy of Gordon and Pat Winchenbach*

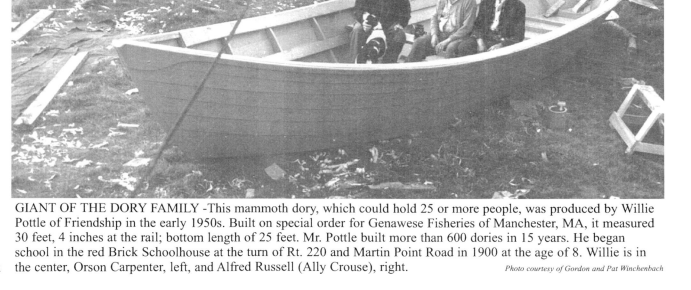

GIANT OF THE DORY FAMILY -This mammoth dory, which could hold 25 or more people, was produced by Willie Pottle of Friendship in the early 1950s. Built on special order for Genawese Fisheries of Manchester, MA, it measured 30 feet, 4 inches at the rail; bottom length of 25 feet. Mr. Pottle built more than 600 dories in 15 years. He began school in the red Brick Schoolhouse at the turn of Rt. 220 and Martin Point Road in 1900 at the age of 8. Willie is in the center, Orson Carpenter, left, and Alfred Russell (Ally Crouse), right. *Photo courtesy of Gordon and Pat Winchenbach*

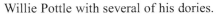

ground, but I'll bet that 1900 was a good year for both of them.

Over the coming years, George and Arvilla lived on the first floor of the house and farmed their land. A large barn was built on one side of the house; a convenience store where they sold produce from their farm, as well as gasoline, was erected on the other. The field was speckled with chicken coops, animal sheds, and gardens, and of course the outhouse. When Willie married Fannie Winchenbaugh in 1915, the house was remodeled, making the upstairs into a separate apartment for the newlyweds. A second story was added to the attached back shed to allow a summer kitchen to be built as part of the apartment, accessed by an outside two-story flight of stairs.

Landscapes have a way of changing over decades, and so it proved true as life at the Pottle homestead shifted from farming to boat building. Willie operated a dory building business on the property that prospered over the years. In 1957 Lew Dietz, who wrote for the *Maine Coast Fisherman,* had this to say, "In the course of the past 20 years, Willie has built more dories than any man in Maine…he's the only builder in Maine commercially engaged in the perpetuation of the Grand Banks dory." A lot of his boats went out of state. "I've been building dories for Boston fishermen for years," Willie said, "and they keep coming back for more…Right now I've got an order from a fellow in Texas. What they do with Bank dories down there is house them over forward and make a well just aft of midships to take a 15-horsepower outboard. What they've got then is a sport tuna boat for around $500. This fellow says it works slick, and he may want plenty more."

After George and Arvilla died, Willie and Fannie, along with their only child, Eleanor, moved to the main floor of the house. The house was spacious for three people; however, the small number of tenants didn't last long. When little Eleanor (later known by townfolks as Mamie) decided to get married, it seemed a little bit like déjà vu.

It seems that Beulah Winchenbach (of Waldoboro) and Elden Cook (of Friendship) had planned to wed on Christmas Eve 1934, at the Baptist Parsonage in Waldoboro. Reverend Horace Taylor was conducting the service and Eleanor and her boyfriend, Kenneth Winchenbach (Beulah's older brother), were to stand up for them. On December 20th, Eleanor had written

in her diary that she and Kenneth "went over to R. R. Collamore's [and] got published to be married in Waldoboro." On the 23rd, she wrote, "Ken came at 3:30. Stayed home in evening…We made wedding plans. Tomorrow nite! [sic]" The next day's entry reads, "Mon. Nothing special in a.m. My Wedding Day. Doesn't seem real. Got reddy [sic] in p.m. Ken came at 5:00. We went up with Beulah + Elden. We surprised [them]. They didn't know about us. We knew about them. Went to Aunt Jule's. Home at 9:00. Slept in spare room." On Christmas day, Eleanor records that Elden and Beulah came to visit. They made ice cream, attended a dance in the evening, had a "good time," she wrote, then added in, "Ken treated on cigars." A thought-provoking notation occurs on December 26th when Eleanor wrote, "Wed. Got up at 8:30. Ken had to go home." On that date she listed the many gifts she received for Christmas and added, "My husband was the best." Further entries suggest that it was a while before Eleanor and Kenneth finally settled down permanently together, phrases like "Ken not down today," or "Ken came in p.m., went home at 1:30." When they finally did move in together, it was here in Friendship living with Eleanor's parents, now a third generation in the home.

Kenneth too was a boat builder. To the several buildings already on the property, he added his own boat shop, used for constructing lobster boats. For many years the Pottle yard was a hub of shipbuilding activity. At some point, Eleanor and her husband moved out of the house to live on their own elsewhere in Friendship; their youngest child, Gwen, moved with them. Their son, Gordon, about 12 at the time, decided to stay and live with his grandparents. Willie died in 1959 and about six years later, Fannie followed, at which time Eleanor inherited the homestead and she and Kenneth moved back in until health required otherwise.

Over the generations, the landscape surrounding the Pottle house has steadily changed. An aerial view postcard of this portion of Martin Point

The George Pottle house in the 1920s.

Photo courtesy of Gordon and Pat Winchenbach

Road shows that at the time George Pottle was settling here, he could look down the hill and see clear out to the *nubbins* (the small islands just off the coastline), hardly a shrub obstructing his view. Today, in winter when all the leaves are down, you can sometimes catch a glimpse of blue shining through the tree trunks. The store was passed on to heirs and served for several years as a summer residence. The structure itself was eventually sold and moved into town. It now forms the basis of the house at the corner of Bradford Point Road and School Street. The barn was razed, and the lumber from it was used by Jim Murphy to build the little house that now sits between the Pottle house and the Friendship Museum. Willie's dory shop is now Winnie Lash's utility building, located just beside the Martin Point Public Landing at the bottom of the hill. Willie probably doesn't mind now its being so close to the water! Chicken coops and pig sheds? Who knows when they all disappeared. The outhouse was toted away in 1981 when central heat and plumbing were installed in the house, and in the fall of 2005, Kenneth's boat shop was burned to the ground.

Although Gordon lived out of state, he visited the homestead year-round, maintaining the house and property. The old garage was preserved, and about 1985 he hired George C. Hall to create the pond that now covers much of the back field. In 2000 Gordon and his wife, Pat, moved to Friendship to live. They made several changes to the house, including adding a fireplace, where there had never been one, and a two-car garage. Even with these added features, their goal was to preserve the outside appearance of the structure. "We like to compare pictures taken of our grandchildren on the sunporch," Pat said, "to pictures of Eleanor and Kenneth, Fannie and Willie, Gordon and Gwen, on the same front porch and know that this is still George Pottle's home away from the sea. The lighthouse weathervane on the peak of the roof reminds us how it all came to be."

The A. Dwight Wotton and George Pottle houses, early 1900s.

Photo courtesy of Penobscot Marine Museum

The George Pottle house in 2006.

Photo by Gordon Winchenbach

30 *Kerr Eby House* By Linda S. DeRosa

An atmosphere of rebellion had arisen in the 13 New England colonies in 1775. During this time of revolutionary fervor, on the fourth day of the month of August "in the fifteenth year of his Majesty's Reign A.D. 1775,"[1] we find Benjamin Wotton of Beverly in the County of Essex in the province of Massachusetts Bay, a mariner, purchasing land from a husbandman, Paul Minch, of Waldoboro in the County of Lincoln of the province of Massachusetts Bay in New England. The purchase of 93 acres in Medumcook (sic) was paid for in the King's currency "the sum of thirteen pounds six shillings and eight pence lawful money, for property described as follows:

"…A Lot of Land lying and being in Medumcook (sic) butted and bounded as followeth, viz, beginning at a spruce tree standing on the Eastern side of Goose River Bay, and from thence running Southeast, three hundred & twenty Poles to a spruce tree standing on the Eastern side of Goose River Bay or Sound said Tree is marked on four sides, and from thence running Southeast, three hundred & twenty Poles to a Spruce tree marked on four sides thence running Southwest fifty poles to a white ash tree, marked on four sides thence running northwest two hundred and seventy poles to said Goose River Sound to a Spruce tree marked, on four sides, then running northerly to the Bounds first mention to contain ninety three Acres and eighty square Poles with the Ledges and without the Ledges there is eighty acres and eighty square Poles as appears by Nath'l Meservey's Plan (sic) said Lot joining Southerly on Micajah Drinkwater Lot and Northerly on John Foglers Lot."[2]

Many sources were utilized while searching for the history and fortunes of the Benjamin Wotton family in Friendship. Bits and pieces

The Kerr Eby house in summer 2006.

Photo by Polly Jones

were extracted from Wotton oral history, and other nuggets were located in *Reconds of Meduncook Plantation and Friendship, Maine 1762-1899.* Editors Ruth J. Aiken and Arthur P. Spear mention in the editors' preface that Meduncook Plantation and Friendship town records were destroyed in a house fire in the early 1900s, so there were many missing pieces.[3] Benjamin Wotton is listed in the 1790 U.S. Census as the head of family with two other males over the age of sixteen, five males under the age of sixteen, and three females of all ages.[4] This being the case, if one of the three females was his wife, Benjamin had a great start to a large family with nine children, and seven of those being male. Wotton family oral history places the antiquity of the Eby house to 1790 with the builder being Benjamin Wotton I. This same history states there was a possibility of an earlier house on the same foundation and that fire burned most of it.[5]

The Records of Meduncook Plantation compiled by Melville B. Cook advises us as to happenings in the early 1800s. By 1804, roads were being surveyed in the Plantation of Meduncook. Benjamin Wotton II evidentially was of adequate means and property to need a bridle road laid out between his home and that of his father's house.[6] Benjamin Wotton was chosen as surveyor for Hatchet Cove on April 7, 1806, and on February 25, 1807, he was chosen for the school committee. Mr. Wotton had an interest in education, as it was voted on October 16, 1807, to hold school in his home for three months during the ensuing winter for one dollar per month.[7] By 1844, Cook records that in May Benjamin Wotton purchased stock and farm implements as well as hay from John Condon.[8] The generations of Wottons have marched steadily on from Nathaniel Wotton, who married Thankful Jameson of Cushing on February 14, 1827,[9] and to others in the family with names of William, Benjamin, and Simeon.[10] A cemetery still exists located on the original Wotton estate property purchased by Benjamin Wotton I. Due to deterioration and disrepair, the Wotton genealogy contained on the

Windowbox on Kerr Eby house, summer 2006.　　　*Photo by Polly Jones*

stones is nearly lost to present-day descendants.

In more recent times, at least since 1933, part of the Wotton estate was purchased by the nationally prominent etcher Kerr Eby. The picturesque waterfront homesite became a perfect place for Mr. Eby to create his etchings, write, and to have a lifestyle that would enhance his artistic productivity.

Mr. Eby was born in 1890 in Tokyo, Japan, the son of Methodist missionaries from Canada. He spent his childhood and youth surrounded by artists and applied his artistic interests as a printer's

Kerr Eby in WWI uniform.

Photo courtesy of Friendship Museum

apprentice in a newspaper office. He moved to New York City and continued his training in art at the Pratt Institute and was employed by the American Lithographic Company as a magazine illustrator.

In 1917, when the United States entered World War I, Eby joined the U.S. Army. Unable to obtain a commission as an artist, he was assigned ambulance duty and later served as a camouflager to the 40th Engineers in France. He did not neglect his art but recorded what he experienced during the war, and when he returned to New York City, he produced powerful prints throughout the 1920s and 1930s reflecting the horrors of war that had impacted him so personally.

Eby's experience in World War I not only affected his art but helped shape his views of the world. In the mid-1930s, world conflict began to erupt, suggesting another world war was in the making. In 1936 Eby produced a book titled *War,* which included works produced from his war experiences. Although he was not strictly a pacifist, he wanted to educate the public to the horrible consequences that war unleashes.[11] On May 30, 1936, the newspaper *Norwalk Hour* ran a front-page article titled "*Battle For Peace Says Man Who Saw Horrors of War.*" In the interview the reporter records that Mr. Eby appealed to the women of the world to stop the coming war, saying: "You women, I am speaking wholly to you now. Is it not possible somehow to get together in your millions and raise hell about this thing all over the world? You could be irresistible. We males, most of us, in this kind of thing are handicapped. It is the tradition of the race that we should be bold. We are afraid to be afraid or to seem afraid. You women have no such inhibitions. You don't have to be men. You don't have to be brave gentlemen; and, if you are moved enough, you don't even have to be ladies. Can't you be afraid enough for your own sons to do something…?"[12]

Mr. Eby tried to enlist when the United States declared war in 1941 but was turned down because of his age. He did serve through a program developed by Abbott Laboratories called the combat artist program. He traveled with the marines in the South Pacific and witnessed the landing of the American invasion force at Tarawa, living three weeks in a foxhole on Bougainville. He became ill with a tropical disease while on Bougainville and returned to the United States unable to regain his full strength. He completed his final drawings for Abbott but died in Norwalk, Connecticut, in 1946 with unfinished etchings he had planned to do from his war pictures.

While residing in Friendship, Mr. Eby continued his artwork, capturing many local scenes, one of which was a painting of Stillman Havener titled *The Clam Digger Returns*. His etching *Shark Ledges*, shown here and on exhibit at the Friendship Museum, is a location well known to Friendship's lobstermen.

The Wotton/Eby legacy is now in the hands of Jon and Celeste Prime, who have embraced the beauty of the land and the home's rich history. During the last few years, improvements have been made to the house by attaching the separate cabin to the main house and adding a living room designed by architect Christopher Glass. The old barn, which possibly served as a Kerr Eby studio, now watches Celeste as she creates works of art from natural native foliage and homegrown floral accents. The Prime family includes three daughters with a number of grandchildren. Before moving to Friendship, Jon, who grew up in Eastport, Maine, called his father and said he was moving back to Maine, reconnecting with his roots. He advised that he was moving his family to Kittery Point. Jon's father reminded his son that he still had some further work to do, Kittery Point being just over the Maine-New Hampshire border, saying, "That's not Maine, that's Boston!"[13] I expect Jon's father is happy now, as Friendship is a classic example of the coast of Maine.

Kerr Eby etching, *Shark Ledges*.   *Etching courtesy Friendship Museum*

Kerr Eby house in summer 2006.

Photo by Polly Jones

31 *James & Hannah Condon Home* By Walter Foster

In 1844 a marriage took place on Loud's Island between Hannah Yates Oram of the island and James Condon 2nd* of Hatchet Cove, Friendship.[1] James had been in the habit of rowing to the island on Sundays while he was courting Hannah, a distance of more than five miles each way.

After the marriage, the young couple resided in Friendship at the farm of James's father, William, on Condon's Head.[2] James continued in the family occupations of fishing, farming, and smacking to Boston. When the Brick Schoolhouse was opened in 1850, Hannah became its first teacher at a wage of one dollar a week.[3] By that time, she already had two of what would become a family of six children.

In May 1858, as recorded in the family Bible, James and Hannah and four children moved into a new house on Hatchet Cove, the house

*This is how James designated himself, i.e., not James II.

that is pictured here. Samuel Brown of Friendship, a master carpenter, built it for them for wages of one dollar a day and his board. A smaller house existing on the property was taken down, and any sound lumber was used in building the new house. James designed and drew up the plans for the house and worked on building it with Samuel.[4] A barn also on the property was retained and is still in use.

On the farm, the Condons kept cows, oxen, and sheep. Henhouses have come and gone, including one in the ell of the house. By the time of this 1898 photo, the original ell had been doubled in length to accommodate an indoor privy, a back stairs to the "porch chamber," and probably the dormer window. Adams Lawry made this addition when he married James and Hannah's daughter Emma in 1879.[5] In the 1930s the ell was again reconfigured for the installation of a modern bathroom. The original small window to the left of the door was replaced by the two standard windows seen there today.

Hannah Condon with her son, Rufus, circa 1898.

Photo courtesy Foster family collection

In the 1880s, when son Willie Everett married, "a shed with a kitchen and sleeping rooms above" was added to the rear north corner of the house. He and his wife and two young sons lived there for a few years. She developed a nice strawberry bed behind the house.[6]

The original well, dug behind the house, was served by a well sweep. Well sweeps, once common in Friendship, give a mechanical assist in filling and raising buckets of water. Later, with the coming of electricity, a pipe brought water from this well into the cellar by an electric pump. In the 1930s a new well was blasted within nearby ledge and similarly piped to the house. By the early 1960s, the family found the need to drill a 245-foot well served by a submersible pump.

The well sweep survives, however, or more accurately, the most recent of a succession of replicas. In the 1920s James and Hannah's youngest, Rufus Condon, built his new home across the road near his boat shop. He discovered that for drinking he preferred the water at the farm to that from the well at his house. As late as the 1940s, when he was in his eighties, Rufus was still walking up to the old well and carrying two buckets of water down to this home. The well sweep is as useful today, if needed, as it was to Rufus and to the new family in 1858.

The house originally had three chimneys for stoves for heating and, in the ell, cooking. The middle chimney was removed in 1974. The other two are still in use.

During the farm years, a north corner of the granite cellar cooled by the evaporation of water springing through the walls served as the milk room.

The Condon house in 1961.

Photo by Bill Cook

The space was fitted with shelves and used for storing milk and butter.

Hannah and James had an oxcart, but they did not keep a horse. In later years, after their daughter Emma and Adams Lawry built a house next door, they sometimes borrowed a horse and cart from them.[7] People got around on foot or by boat. It wasn't until the 1920s that a garage was added on to the far side of the barn to house an automobile.

After moving into their new home in 1858, Hannah and James Condon lived on their farm for the remainder of their lives. In the 1898 photo, Hannah was a recent widow. Her son Randall Condon, an educator living out of state, was returning with his family for summer visits at his childhood home. Son Rufus and his wife lived at the farm from 1910 to 1913, taking care of it and Hannah during her final years. During this period, the addition on the rear of the house provided Hannah her own apartment and entry during her vigorous old age.[8] After her death in 1911, this addition was removed and became part of a residence elsewhere in town.

Randall Condon and his wife, Eliza Sturtevant Condon, who was called Lydie, took over the property in 1913 and lived there seasonally and in retirement. During the years until his death in 1931, Randall and others in his family played a major role in restoring the Roadside Cemetery and forming the Friendship Village Society, an early initiative of which was to purchase land for a playground for the new village school when it replaced the Brick Schoolhouse in 1922.[9]

Randall's sentimental purchase of the Brick Schoolhouse, where both he and his mother had taught, made it available as a regular meeting place for community groups and led to its use as the Friendship Museum years later and the gift of the building to the museum in 2005 by Randall's grandson Randall Foster.

Randall and Lydie made many plantings and oversaw the transition of the homestead from working farm to country home. It was one of the last houses around to become electrified because Randall was reluctant to leave behind the warm glow of the kerosene lamp. Randall and Lydie also added the green shutters and the rose arbor over the front door, which gave the house the cottage look captured in this 1942 photograph. In 1947 the property passed to their only child, Katharine Foster, and her husband, Frank Foster. For a time, once again, the family used it as a summer home. Frank added a wide dormer

window at the rear of the house, which brought light into the "dark bedroom" and to other space as well.

Katharine and Frank Foster's son Walter Foster and his wife, Carolyn Foster, have made the place their year-round home since 1967.

Hand-tinted photo of the Condon house in summer 1942.

Hand-tinted by Sherman Wotton

The James and Hannah Condon home in summer 2006.

Photo by Walter Foster

32 The Samuel Lawry House By Linda S. DeRosa

Lawry generations have been recorded in New England since 1630. Sailing from East Anglia, England, the first Lawrys arrived in the Boston area in the wave of immigration that occurred that year. In 1657 Cornelius Lawry is reported to have been a domestic employed by Rev. Samuel Dudley, a resident of Exeter, New Hampshire.[1] Rev. Dudley was a son of Thomas Dudley, the third governor of Massachusetts.[2]

At a later date Mr. Lawry was appointed hog reeve. Whatever Mr. Lawry's circumstances were early in his life, he was soon able to progress to landowner with purchases in 1664, 1680, and 1681.[3] Three more generations of Lawrys settled in the Exeter, New Hampshire, area with a member of the fourth generation, Samuel Lawry, leaving New Hampshire and moving to the settlement of Meduncook Plantation in 1757.[4] Samuel was among other young men who saw an opportunity to make a new start in a fledgling settlement on the coast of Massachusetts (Maine) in response to an offer by an agent for the Waldo Patent of 1743 seeking twenty pioneer families to settle the Meduncook

The Samuel Lawry house in summer 2006.

Photo by Polly Jones

Plantation. "Pioneers of English stock and Puritan faith could look forward to a plot of 100 acres, with forty rods of frontage on sea or river; it came free, and another adjoining 100 acres were available at a quit-rent of one penny per acre."[5]

As the plantation began to put down permanent roots, the frame house construction by Samuel Lawry was built at Hatchet Cove in 1760. This construction followed closely on the heels of the first frame house built in Meduncook, reported to have been built on Thomas (Davis) Point in 1759. In *The Lawry Family of Friendship, Maine* by A. E. Sutton, two more generations of Lawrys prospered in Meduncook, as did a third begun by James Lawry. James lived from 1804 to 1872 and would have been a three-year-old in 1807 when Meduncook Plantation was incorporated as the town of Friendship. In 1847 a fourth-generation Lawry in Friendship (seventh in New England) came into existence with the birth of Adams Davis Lawry (1849-1913). Adams was born in the original Lawry homestead built by his great-grandfather Samuel Lawry, patriarch of the Friendship Lawrys.

At the early age of twelve Adams went to sea as a cabin boy and by nineteen was a captain. He sailed the East Coast from Nova Scotia to North Carolina, surviving a hurricane during which his ship sank off Virginia. He also lived to tell about being lost for two days as fog descended on his vessel near the Bay of Fundy.[6]

Adams Davis Lawry married Philena Emmaline Condon on November 10, 1879, after his first wife, Mary Rogers, died in childbirth. This seventh-generation family grew to include five children, Melvin, Mary Ada, Oram Robert, Stanley Adams, and Clinton Chamberlain Lawry.

Clinton Chamberlain Lawry, Clinton the first, attended an art school in Boston and obtained his first job with the Hood Rubber Company. His second job was designing and painting commercial billboard art for John W. Donnelly, an outdoor advertising company.[7] Clint's artistic talent can be enjoyed at the Friendship Museum by viewing the two water-colors hanging there depicting the arrival of the steamship *Minneola* and the stepping of a mast on a Friendship sloop. His *Welcome to Friendship* signs were classics. The two most often remembered were the Friendship sloop and the portrait of "Allie" (Albert D. Cushman), a veteran lobsterman of 70 years. He is depicted pointing toward Friendship with a buoy in his hand and stating," 'bout 10 miles that away—Friendship, that is." The subject of the signs would change seasonally, and it was a pleasure to see a new one.

A special painting, a wall mural located in the entry room at the newer Lawry bungalow at Hatchet Cove, reminds the current Lawry generations of their rich heritage. This Clint Lawry I painting is a time capsule of how the artist remembered his father, Captain Adams Davis Lawry. Captain Adams is shown rowing out to a schooner anchored in Hatchet Cove with the Sand islands in the background. Three young boys' heads appear in the foreground, as if sitting on the stern seat of a dory, representing three Lawry brothers, Oram, Stanley, and the artist himself, Clinton I.

The original 1760 homestead passed from Lawry ownership, but in 1958 was purchased and once again owned by a Lawry, Stanley Adams Lawry, an eighth-generation descendant of Cornelius Lawry. Stanley A. Lawry served the town of Friendship as a selectman in the 1970s. Oral tradition, whether accurate or not we are not sure, denotes the existing structure located off of Floods Cove Road as being built on the original 1760 foundation. The original structure burned, suggesting that the present cottage style dwelling is of a more recent vintage.

In 1982 the house was purchased by Marjorie Lewis. Marjorie has modernized the home with very limited changes, retaining original architectural lines and features like the very low ceilings and an

"Allie" (Albert D. Cushman) portrayed by Clint Lawry. *Photo by Warren Conary*

Clint Lawry painting of Captain Adams Davis Lawry rowing the three Lawry brothers: Oram, Stanley, and the artist himself, Clinton I. *Photo by Polly Jones*

exceptionally steep and narrow staircase leading to the upstairs. The home is her summer retreat and occasional rental property. In earlier days there was a clear view to the ocean's edge, and the present road curving north just beyond the house curved south.[8] A display of brilliant cobalt blue bottles on a high shelf in an entrance hallway welcomes guests and friends.

Generations of Lawrys have always found Friendship a good place to be. Currently, members of the Lawry family return to a spacious bungalow style home built in 1920 by Rufus Condon and only a short distance from the original Lawry homestead. Lawry descendents scattered throughout the United States (in California, Colorado, Texas, Ohio, Virginia, New York and New Hampshire) will always return to Friendship to remain connected to their roots and heritage.

Clinton C. Lawry II with sons Clinton Lawry III "Chip" on his right, David Lawry on his left, and Randall Lawry on the lower step.

Photo by Polly Jones

Clinton C. Lawry III with daughter, Cynthia Denio, and grandson, Caleb, a tenth-generation Lawry offspring.   *Photo by Polly Jones*

Clint Lawry I wall mural of the Lawry family tree.   *Photo by Polly Jones*

33 *Cap'n Am's House* By Mary Flood Thompson

This house, now called Cap'n Am's and named for Ambrose Simmons, was built circa 1850 by Seward Poland III. The Polands, according to Edward Poland Jr. of Round Pond, contrary to Dr. Hahn's papers, came from England in 1642, settling in Lynn, Massachusetts.[1] They later moved to the islands of Maine near Hall Island and then came to the mainland, establishing themselves in Friendship. Edward Poland Jr, is the great-great-grandson of Captain Frank Poland.

Nancy Poland married Elbridge Wotton Sr., who died at sea. Later she married Francis Leeman. They continued to live on the property until Mr. Leeman's death. Nancy sold the place to Ambrose Simmons in

Cap'n Am's in summer 2006.

Photo by Chuck Thompson

1865. Ambrose was quite a character, as described by several anecdotes in the records at the library. Ambrose married Mary Francis Burns of Waldoboro after a very short courtship – a funny story also in records at the library. It was a love match that continued until her death in 1897; Ambrose always carried her picture.

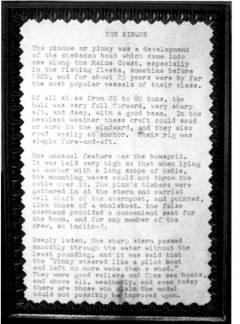

THE PINQUE

The pinque or pinky was a development of the chebacco boat which came into use along the Maine Coast, especially in the fishing fleets, sometime before 1820, and for about 25 years were by far the most popular vessels of their class.

Of all sizes from 20 to 80 tons, the hull was very full forward, very sharp aft, and deep, with a good beam. In the heaviest weather these craft could scud or work to the windward, and they also road easily at anchor. Their rig was simple fore-and-aft.

One unusual feature was the bowsprit. It was laid very high so that when lying at anchor with a long scope of cable, the mounting waves could not throw the cable over it. The pink's timbers were gathered in at the stern and carried well abaft of the sternpost, and pointed, like those of a whaleboat. the false overhand provided a convenient seat for the boom, and for any member of the crew, so inclined.

Deeply laden, the sharp stern passed smoothly through the water without the least pounding, and it was said that the "Pinky steered like a pilot boat and left no more wake than a shad." They were good sailers and fine sea boats, and above all, weatherly, and even today there are those who claim the model could not possibly be improved upon.

Description of a pinkie that accompanies the model of the *Defiance*.

Photo by Chuck Thompson

Ambrose fished off the Grand Banks in his pinkie, which was called the *Defiance,* that now rests on the bottom of the ocean in Hatchet Cove. A pinkie is a double-ended sailing vessel, which took wonderfully to the sea. It could be worked in rougher weather and sailed like a dream. The model shown below is the actual model from which Ambrose's *Defiance* was built circa 1865. For more on the Pinkie design and its history, see the insert. Here is an excerpt taken from the *Fisherman's Memorial*, an 1873 Gloucester, Massachusetts pub-

lication: "These little vessels from their extreme buoyancy and offering so little resistance to the power of the ocean waves, would make comparatively good progress to weather at time when larger ships would be laboring, plunging, and straining every plank and timber to its utmost capacity of endurance. They would mount almost on an even keel upon the crest of the highest seas and settle into the hollows with ease and grace of a wild duck."

Mary and Ambrose raised fourteen children in the story and a half cape, which was what it was at that time. It had a kitchen in the front of the house, so Mary could see Ambrose when he came in from the sea, a small parlor and their bedroom with a fireplace, and an attic where all the children slept. The drainpipe holes are still evident in the floor of one of the bedrooms upstairs (originally Mary's kitchen) as the house was raised to put a first floor under, by Dr. Everett Flood in 1904. Ambrose had become acquainted

Flood's Cove mooring ring for the *Defiance*.

Photo by Carol Hoch

Model of the pinkie, *Defiance*.

Photo by Chuck Thompson

Flood's Cove wharf, home of *Defiance*.

Photo by Chuck Thompson

with Everett Flood when he came to Friendship at the age of twenty to become the schoolteacher in the one-room schoolhouse on Friendship Long Island in 1875. Dr. Flood boarded with Ambrose while teaching school on the island.

Dr. Flood used the money he earned from teaching to go to Bowdoin College to study medicine, graduating in 1881. Later, when he decided to retire, he wanted to come back to Maine. Having loved the cove, Dr. Flood contacted Ambrose. Ambrose said his wife had died and "none of his children seemed to want the place," so he sold it to my grandfather (Dr. Flood) circa 1898. Ambrose went out to Harbor Island, we believe, where he lived out his life. Ambrose died in 1909 and is buried in the Roadside Cemetery with a prominent headstone.

Dr. Flood raised the Cap'n Am's house sometime around 1904 putting a first floor underneath, several fireplaces, and wraparound porches, which

Drawing of the Friendship Long Island schoolhouse interior by George F. Payne.

Photo by Chuck Thompson

have since been glassed in to make a large sleeping porch, with a kitchen, dining room, and library. He lived there until his death in 1937. Dr. Flood is also buried in the Roadside cemetery near Ambrose. The house was raised again in 1995 to put it on a new foundation, as the fireplaces and old rock cellar were crumbling. The house is now secure and will, we hope, stand another hundred years.

The Floods have occupied the property since 1898. Currently, two brothers, John and David Flood, live at the cove with their wives, Marge and Joyce, year-round. Their sister, Mary, and her husband John Thompson, return each summer to fill out the third-generation roster. A fourth and fifth generation of Floods also return to this special corner of Friendship, filling the seaside landscape with joyful laughter and the scampering of youthful feet. Dr. Flood, being the scholar that he was, put up a Latin sign visible as you enter the cove. The sign has greeted all who have wandered down the road for the last 100-plus years. It is a direct quote from Horace, which translated loosely says "TO ME THIS CORNER OF THE EARTH SHINES FORTH ABOVE ALL." This is a feeling we all hold, as Flood's Cove has such a special place in our hearts.

Captain Am's front porch in summer 2006.

Photo by Linda S. DeRosa

Photo courtesy Penobscot Marine Museum

Latin sign at Flood's Cove.

Photo courtesy of Flood family collection

34 Captain Charles Comery Cottage By Ann Martin Filippi

In August 1892 Captain Charles Comery, a Waldoboro resident and a partner in the Crystal Pond Ice Company, purchased a cottage lot from Leonard Condon. Between 1892 and the early 1900s, several additional lots were carved from the Condon property, and the summer cottages along Richards Point Lane were constructed.

When the original Comery cottage was built in 1895 and then the barn in 1896, the old Martin Point Road crossed the adjoining property to the west (site of the present tennis court) and then continued up the hill past the Armstrong property; therefore, the sliding barn door, which today faces the ocean, was adjacent to the old road. In the early 1900s the state allocated money for a wider section of road to be built closer to Crystal Pond, in a flat but rather marshy area. To access the cottage from the new Martin Point Road, the Comerys and their successors used a ten-foot wide path, just about enough for a horse and buggy and later for an early automobile, registered as 56-026 Maine 1923. Since an early postcard identifies this section of Martin Point as Richards Point, most likely from the Richards boarding house next door to the Comery cottage, today the access road is called Richards Point Lane.

When Charles Comery died, he left the cottage to his daughter, Ida Willey, and her husband, Roby. Subsequently, upon Roby's death in 1931, the property passed to Leola Oliver, Glenys Burnheimer's mother. Glenys and her husband acquired the property from Leola in 1937. When Glenys died in 1984, her daughter, Ruth Burnheimer Teague, inherited the property and two years later, in 1986, sold it to Ann Martin Filippi, the current owner.

The original style and appearance of the cottage was a type of folk house, typical of the structure imported by the first colonists from England. Built directly on the ground of a heavy timber frame with hewn-and-pegged joints and covered with board and batten, it had a highly pitched front-gabled roof, which made the structure one and one-half stories high—the area under the roof, i.e., the half-story, accessed by ladder. The hand-hewn floor joists hung from the frame—unsupported below.

Captain Charles Comery cottage in summer 2006.

Photo by Elaine Lang Cornett

A careful look at the roof and walls of the original structure reveals these early features, which also include some eighteen-inch roof boards.

Most likely, local materials were used, transported by water to the dock at the ice house. Subsequently, exterior shed-roof type alterations provided additional living space. The kitchen and dining area was added as a lean-to attached to one side of the house, and later another lean-to on the opposite side added a small bathroom and extended a first floor bedroom. These additions are easily recognized because the exterior and roof line of the original house remain as one wall.

Located on a high section of ground with a long view of Muscongus Bay, the house faces due southwest and therefore receives the prevailing summer southwesterly breezes. With the exception of a wharf built in 2003, the property remains essentially the same as in 1986 when it was purchased by Ann Filippi.

Postcard showing the Comery cottage on Richards Point. *Courtesy of Ann Filippi*

Rock pile remains of ice house wharf (beyond Ann Filippi's wharf) on Martin Point. *Photo by Elaine Lang Cornett*

Interior of the cottage, looking out to the end of Martin Point. *Photo by Elaine Lang Cornett*

35 *The Pond House* By David Adams Hovell

Warranty deed dated December 16, 1880, Knox County Registry of Deeds, recorded in book 56, page 534, from Leonard Condon and Elizina Condon, wife, to Charles Comery et al.: "Know all Men by these Presents that I, Leonard Condon, of Friendship, in the County of Knox and State of Maine, in consideration of the sum of three hundred seventy five dollars, paid by the parties & in the amounts as follows, to wit: Nelson Thompson, Zenos Cook, John R. Studley, Eli Bickmore, each fifty dollars, Franklin Thompson, N.W. Thompson, and Orrin W. Condon each twenty five dollars and all of said Friendship, Frank A. Hutchings and Charles Comery both of Waldoboro each fifty dollars."

Thus began the commercial venture of the Crystal Lake Ice Company. The company built the Pond House next to the lake, an ice house east of the current road, and a pier whose end footing can still be seen offshore. I have several photos of the ice-cutting operation and the pond end of the ice slide which, carried the ice to the ice house for storage. One shows Alason Wotton maneuvering a block of ice to the start of the slide. The block of ice in this photo appears to be crystal clear. I have been told that, because of the shallow depth of the pond, the ice often had vegetation in it, and thus was not of top quality. I have not been able to determine when the ice operation ended. I have several rent receipts from just before 1900, which would indicate that the ice company was no longer using the Pond House to house workers. One dated Oct. 17, 1899, reads, "Received from A E Wotton fifteen Dollars for rent of Cottage at Martins Point for the season of 1899, signed L J Turner." In Hattie M. Wotton's *The Memories of an Old Parlor Set and My Childhood Days 1817-1947,* she writes, "We moved to Tiverton, R.I. and the following winter he contracted LaGrippe. It left him so deaf he had to give up his position, much to our sorrow and disappointment. We came home and started the ice business (there was also a pond behind Stanley and Priscilla Simmons' house) and made many friends among the summer residents. Our daughter (Nellie Frances Wotton) followed in

The Pond House in summer 2006.

Photo by Elaine Lang Cornett

my footsteps and became one of the outstanding educators in New England, and our son (Alason Dwight) helped us at home and took over the ice business."

The Pond House was built from wood cut on the lot, rough-sawed pine boards of the type commonly used at that time. The floorboards are wide, some fifteen inches in width, and are nailed with homemade square iron nails. Over the years the nails have rusted until each one now has a black ring around the nailhead and as the green wood dried, a wide crack was left between the floorboards. The floors are pitted with tiny holes from the crampons on the soles of the workers' boots. The crampons were to keep the men from falling when they went out on the ice.

The ceiling is made of narrow boards twenty-four feet long and the walls have horizontal boards. The stairs to the second floor were so steep that it was like climbing a ladder. The builder did not bother to cut them evenly, just hit or miss, and the treads were only four or five inches wide. They were really dangerous unless one went down backward as on a ladder. There were large double beds in each corner of the second floor. A big black iron stove served to heat the house and cook the food.

The Pond House was the original location of the Martin, Maine, Post Office, founded in 1890 through the efforts of Miss Etta Glidden and Herbert Weaver. Nellie Brazier and her mother, Hattie, were the first postmistresses. Years later the post office moved next door into the community house, until its closing in the 1970s.

After the demise of the Crystal Lake Ice Company, the house, as a cottage, was occupied in the summer by Captain Alason E. Wotton, his wife, Hattie, and their family. After the death of her father and mother, Nellie Wotton Brazier stayed in the house as her summer cottage until her more modern place, the Bos'n Locker, was built across the road.

Nellie sold the Pond House in 1964 to the present owner, David Adams Hovell Jr., whose parents used it as a summer cottage. In the summers of 1965 and 1966, David and his father did extensive structural repairs to the building. This involved jacking up the house off the six rocks it rested upon and inserting cement posts. All of the original narrow clapboard was replaced with new, replicating the original. All new 6-over-6 windows with headers were fabricated in Rockland. While many improvements have been made, the Pond House still retains its old charm.

Postcard photo of the ice house. *Courtesy of Friendship Museum*

Pond House, view from pond side with gas light, seated female and buggy.
Photo courtesy David Hovell © 2006 David Hovell

Remains of the pier from the Crystal Lake Ice Company. *Photo by Elaine Lang Cornett*

The Hovells lived in Bloomfield, New Jersey. Winifred Emmeline Paterson Hovell grew up in South Paris, Maine. David Adams Hovell Sr. was from Forfar, Angus, Scotland. They continued to summer in the Pond House into their nineties.

In 2005-2006, the garage, which had been flooded by the increased level of Crystal Pond, was removed and the deck enlarged and screened. Now retired, David Jr. and David C. Frost are continuing the fifty-year tradition of summers in the Pond House. For the balance of the year, they live in Dover, Pennsylvania.

Ice cutting, view from ice ramp with six men and two horses.

Photo courtesy David Hovell © 2006 David Hovell

Edith's Maine Baked Beans

Edith Emmeline Emerson Paterson
(1874–1960)

2 pounds dried navy beans
Water
1-pound salt pork cut in one-inch cubes
1 onion
3/4 cup unsulphured molasses, plus 1/4 cup brown sugar
Or
1 cup unsulphured molasses, plus 1-1/2 teaspoons dry mustard
Boiling water.

The Day Before:

Pick over beans and wash well. Place beans in non-aluminum bowl, covering beans with several inches of cold water.

The Next Morning:

In a heavy non-aluminum four-quart pot that can be used in oven, put cubed salt pork, beans and soaking water – bring to a boil, then lower heat and simmer until, when blowing on a bean, the skin splits. This will be 60 to 90 minutes, depending on how hard or slow the beans are simmered.

Preheat oven to 250 degrees F

Add the remaining ingredients and stir, adding boiling water to just cover beans.

Place in oven, bake for 8 hours, stir now and then, add boiling water to keep beans submerged.

Note: Edith Emmeline Emerson Paterson's family lived in Maine since before the Revolutionary War. She was related to Ralph Waldo Emerson and to George Emerson, a founder of the Canadian Cattle Industry in Calgary, Alberta, and grandmother to David Hovell, current owner of the Pond House.

Hauling block of ice up ramp, group of six men.

Photo courtesy David Hovell © 2006 David Hovell

VII East Friendship

Meduncook (Friendship) River vista in winter, looking upriver toward Salt Pond in East Friendship.

Photo by Stephen T. Hensel

36 *The Zebulon Davis House* By Kathy MacLeod

The Elizabeth and Zebulon Davis house in East Friendship has been a farm to many families for over 200 years. It initially included a large section of land running down to the Back River and up and over the ridge in the front of the house. Like many of the original homes in Friendship, it was a center-chimney Cape Cod. The opening to the original chimney is still visible in two of the rooms in the original part of the house. Evidence of the original structure appears in the attic, where the purlins and rafters are still visible along with hand-hewn beams with wooden pegs. The decking in the attic is 80% original with rough-sawn boards. It appears that the center portion on the original chimney collapsed in the mid 1890's. Some of the original bricks were reused on a second chimney in what later would become the present day kitchen.

Over the decades the house has had it's deed transferred over twelve times, and at least once the house was used as a store— in the late 1880s. Harold and Ruby Allen lived in the house in the 1920s and 1930s, during the depression years. Times were difficult during those years just keeping food on the table. One night in December 2000 we were lucky enough to meet one of the Allens' nieces who actually lived in our home for a short time. She knocked on our door to tell us how happy she was to see the old house so festively decorated for Christmas. She told us that one of her first memories as a child was of celebrating Christmas in the house. She was living with her Aunt Ruby for a while, and she remembered Uncle Harold making a trip to Waldoboro to pick up the Christmas presents that had come in on a train from Boston. She remembers it as one of her best Christmas times ever inside the cozy warm house. I was so surprised by the visit that I never even thought to ask her name until after they had driven off.

The Zebulon Davis house in Winter 2007.

Photo by Susan Lott

Over the years I have heard many stories from several townspeople who as children had walked up to the house to purchase fresh picked strawberries and blueberries from a widow and her daughter who lived here in the 1940s and 1950s. Charles and Rena Fales purchased the farm in 1938.

Al and Betty Roberts carried on the farming tradition during the 1950s through the 1970s, raising sheep and cattle on the farm. The first time I met Betty Roberts, she took me aside to tell me about the night her sheep broke out of their pen and she went out looking for them in her nightie. With a flashlight in hand she spotted them across the road, standing on a large rock. As she was crossing the road, she realized the town constable was driving his nightly rounds and coming right toward her! Not wanting to be seen in her nightclothes out chasing her sheep, she dove into some bushes to hide while he drove past, thus avoiding an embarrassing encounter. Betty always had some amusing story about the farm every time I ran into her around town. It was obvious that she loved her years farming here.

Over the years most of the old farms sold off acreage, as they needed more money and less land for livestock, and this farm was no different. It appears from the Knox County Registry of Deeds that the farm started with about 150 acres and has gone down to two acres.[1] We believe that the barn that currently stands on the property was not the original barn but, rather, part of another barn reassembled on the property in the last 100 years. Some of the timbers have been numbered, and we also found an old headboard for a bed with a shipment tag on it from Easter Island.

The barn was in terrible shape when we arrived and probably should have been torn down, but the more we explored the barn, the more we realized that it had as much history as the house. It obviously had housed sheep, cows, chickens, pigs, and horses over the years. A household 100 years ago would have needed all of these to maintain itself in food for sale and personal use. Only one sill was actually supporting the barn weight, and none of the beams connected to the sill, so we have still never figured out what was keeping it standing upright.

My husband, Ken, attached a come-along winch and many guide wires and slowly jacked the easternmost corner of the barn 1/8 of an inch a day until he had moved it a total of 9-1/2 inches back into position. The barn would creak horribly if he moved it too far too quickly, almost like a 100-year-old person getting up out of a chair after 50 years. It took over a year, but the barn currently has running water and electricity and is back to housing livestock. When you open the big sliding doors in the front of the barn and hear the horses whinny for breakfast, you can feel that the barn is complete again.

From the moment we moved into this old house, it has felt like home. We've added rooms and made our own improvements, as all the owners of the home have done in the past. We currently have ducks and chickens on the property along with the horses. We built a greenhouse down by the garden so we could extend our growing season. When I'm out in the garden and unearth a piece of a crockery from over 100 years ago, I am reminded that we are but a small part of our home's history.

Molly MacLeod and Alfie. *Photo by Kathy MacLeod*

Mortise and tenon and hewn timbers in the attic of the Zebulon Davis house.

Photos by Ken MacLeod

Betty and Al Roberts with their sheep at the Union Fair. *Photo courtesy of Nancy Penniman*

Ken MacLeod on the roof of the barn in 2003. *Photo by Kathy MacLeod*

37 *Hjalmer Autio Farm* By *Marguerite C. Sylvester*

Driving along Route 97 your attention is drawn in the spring to a colorful patch of lupines (or in the fall to the firebush with its brilliant red leaves) on the side of a drive to a home weathered to a rich silver patina on the knoll . You might question, "Why? Why is this home important?" Considered to be one of the oldest homesteads in East Friendship, it demands your attention. Greater yet, it is like a "chrysalis" with marvelous stories developing within its walls; stories of hardy pioneers, tenacious farmers, and staunch families.

Early maps of Friendship indicate this was Davis property. Searching through the deeds you will find the names of Elisha Davis, farmer, and Samuel Davis, who purchased this farm in 1837 from Thurston Jameson, son of Paul Jameson, one of the earliest settlers of Medumcook.

Down through the years, there have been a variety of owners. In 1924, it was sold to Benjamin Lakso, who in turn sold the land to Hjalmar Autio in 1926. At that time, it became a working farm, the

Vieno on swing. *Photo courtesy of Autio Family*

Autio farm, a farm with roots in Finland, a farm with a story to tell.

Ahti Autio shares with us that his father, Hjalmar Autio, left Finland in 1904, coming to America to start a new life. Arriving in Boston, Massachusetts, he settled in Quincy, Massachusetts where he worked in a quarry. Drawn to Friendship by friends, John and Maria Johnson of Cushing, and "yearning to breathe free", he moved his family to Friendship, Maine.[1] Let's capture a taste of life on a farm, through the eyes of Hjalmar's daughter, Vieno Autio:

"In 1926 Father bought the tidewater farm in East Friendship (where Nancy Penniman now lives) and moved his family there from Quincy, Massachusetts. There were eight of us—father Hjalmar, mother Elina, my three older brothers Aimo, Waino, Walter, and my older sister,

The Hjalmer Autio Farm in Fall 2006

Photo by Elaine Lang Cornett

Evelyn. Our oldest brother, Harry, stayed in Quincy, as he had a job there. I remember we traveled to Rockland by boat. How we got to the farm with bag and baggage is a mystery. I was only three years old! Probably that was accomplished with the help of the many Finnish people who lived in the area.[2]

The farmhouse we moved into was supposed to be one of the oldest houses in Friendship. There was a big ell kitchen, comfortable living room, three bedrooms, and a bed in the unfinished attic plus two back pantries and a dirt-floored cellar. There was a pump at the kitchen sink, an Aladdin lamp, and kerosene lamps for light. We had a black iron wood stove for heat and cooking. There will never be another stove like that blessed kitchen range that radiated so much warmth and comfort in that first cold and snowiest winter. Also there was a pot-bellied stove in one of the bedrooms.

There must have been stock (animals) on the farm already when we moved there, because I always remember it as a working farm from day one. When you went in through the big barn doors, there was a big black bull with a ring through his nose in the first stall. (I was always afraid of that bull.) On the same side there were about twelve cows in their own stalls with automatic water cups. At the back there was a room for the new calves. I loved those cows and their babies.

On the left side of the barn floor was the grain room as you entered. There were three big wooden bins with bran and feed for the cows and oats for the horses. The bran was delicious. Then there was an alcove and a door at the back to the horse stalls for the two big farm horses. There were windows in front of their stalls.

We also raised rabbits for a while, but I think they multiplied too fast. There was a huge loft full of hay, a wonderful place to play. Father built a long henhouse; that was more successful than rabbits. He crated the eggs and took them to Rockland. I remember a separate brooder house with a round galvanized stove to keep the baby chicks warm when we got a new lot in the spring. I remember a few ducks too, but we never had roast duck.

The first thing father and the boys built was a Finnish sauna (steam bath) with a wood stove and heated stones for steam, just as they had in

Finland. That was our Saturday night's adventure after the week's work was done.

Autio farm in winter 1938. *Photo courtesy of Autio Family*

Father had a milk route. Every morning he would go in an old-fashioned blue panel truck and deliver milk, cream, and vegetables to all his customers, including summer people. Older people in the village have told me they still remember him.

The farm was busy place year-round. We always had two big gardens, one for vegetables and one for potatoes, enough to last us all year. After the planting came the haying (at least two crops). It was fun to jump on the hay to press it down (kid's job). Then the root crops and the apples had to be harvested. Of course, Mother canned everything she could lay her hands on. In the dirt-floor cellar was a big wooden bin of potatoes, barrels of apples, and shelves full of canned fruit and vegetables. Oh yes, crocks of butter. It was my job to churn the round wood churn whenever we had extra cream, especially in the spring when the cows would freshen after calving.

In the fall Father and the boys would work in the wood lot, cutting wood and hauling it out on the pung. There was some kind of saw machine with a gas engine that they used to cut the wood into stove lengths. Then it was stored in the woodshed (that shed is still standing).

Of course, father was luckier than some. My four brothers were his farm help. They all worked hard from morning to night. I don't remember any of them going on strike, although they probably felt like it at times! Just taking care of the animals was a big job every day in the year. I can remember going to the barn on beautiful summer mornings

Aimo and Waino plowing with horses, Skip and Jim. *Photo courtesy of Autio Family*

Ahti Autio and Arnold Autio driving the cows back to the barn.
Photo courtesy of Autio Family

when he started milking before 6:00 a.m.

My two younger brothers were born here. Ahti in December 1927 and Arnold in May 1931. I can remember the night Ahti was born. He was lying on a white pillow in the black captain's chair. I was sitting there watching him. I was so thrilled to have a baby brother!

Well, the great day arrived. We left the nineteenth century and entered into the twentieth. We were connected to electricity! About 1928 we had electric lights, a water pump, a faucet at the kitchen sink instead of a hand pump! Miracle of all, an electric wringer washer. Of course, it was still back-breaking work. We rinsed in two tubs on a bench in the middle of the kitchen floor. Everything went through the wringer three times, but it was a great improvement over the washboard and the big copper boiler on the kitchen stove! The whole wash was hung out winter and summer. I learned young how to iron shirts, lots of shirts. The electricity helped in the dairy too. Father had a cement cooler, also a bottle washing machine and a cream separator. And no more lanterns in the barn."

An interview with Arnold Autio[3] drew forth other precious memories, nostalgic memories, of catching smelts at night in Arthur Orne's brook, fishing with four hooks at once, digging clams on the shore, and being amazed by all those horseshoe crabs in the river.

For a moment, Arnold was back at the farm on a spring morning, breathing in the fragrance of the abundant apple blossoms in the apple orchard in the front yard. Seconds later, he was chuckling over the fact that he was only eight years old when he harnessed the horses, Skip and Jim, to the rake and was raking hay for the farm. (One learns responsibility early when you live on a farm.)

Arnold, like Vieno, recalled that in preparation for winter the cellar would contain a crock of butter, another of sauerkraut, a barrel of cider, and bin of potatoes. The boys had the task of milking the cows. As Arnold milked the cows, often the cats would line up to get a squirt of milk directed at them straight from the teat. Once milking was complete, often the boys would help churn the cream to make butter. Homemade ice cream was one of the rewards of living on the farm. It was not all work, although when questioned about holidays on the farm, Arnold retorted, "There are no holidays on the farm."

It is so easy to take for granted the modern conveniences that we have. Life was not always easy for those who lived here, but it was rich with love and shared relationships. It is good to remember the values, the hard work, and the tenacity that our forebears represent and to have a greater appreciation for the contribution they made and the heritage they left us.

After the Autios moved away, one might wonder, "What next?"

During WWII, Robert Armstrong Sr. moved two old grinding wheels from the remains of a one hundred and fifty year old mill at the Friendship/Cushing bridge and renamed it Mill Wheel Farm. Here he raised turkeys with Albert Jameson supervising the project.[4]

A few years later as folks traveled along Route 97, the farm became a subject of intense interest. Those who passed by came to a halt to stare with amazement, not at Hjalmar's complacent cows, but at four-legged, long-horned, redheads, a "fold" of Scottish Highland longhorn cattle, cattle with their long horns and very shaggy pelts grazing on the side of the knoll, cattle requiring only hay and a quart of grain a day, cattle who could stay outdoors year round. Robert Armstrong Jr. proclaimed, "They, with all their strength,

Scottish Highland longhorn cattle.

Photo courtesy of Nancy Penniman

owned the farm" and sometimes more. Sue Armstrong recalled, "They were definitely not gentle and friendly. Occasionally, they would break out, and I would receive calls from concerned neighbors reporting, 'Your cows are looking in my window and I cannot get out of my house.'"[5]

Today, the home is important because of the people who live there, their strength, their persistence, their compassion. We find Nancy Penniman,[6] the present owner, braiding together colorful harmonious strands of woolen cloth, creating a beautiful braided rug. In the kitchen with its wide floorboards, Nancy recalled searching for a home in Maine as her husband, Arthur, neared retirement age. When he found a job at Sears, Roebuck in Rockland, Maine, they moved onto the farm that extended from Back River across Route 97 and a mile through the woods to the Goose River.

As the home had deteriorated during the period when no one lived there, the Pennimans spent many days restoring the home to its original beauty. Arthur's handiwork is revealed by the many improvements he made.

As Nancy graciously gives you a tour, she points out the exposed "gunstock studs," joweled corner posts, wide at the top and narrow at the bottom to provide more room for intersecting joints. They are an indication that the age of the home dates back to the eighteenth century.

Nancy Penniman creating braided rugs. *Photo by Elaine Lang Cornett*

38 *The Cornelius Bradford House— A Homestead with Pioneer Roots* *By Marguerite C. Sylvester*

Stalwart pioneers of the Massachusetts Bay Colony came by sea (Indian trails and waterways were the avenues of transportation at that time) and settled in a place called Meduncook in the early 1700s. Let's examine some of those who led the way, familiar names in the annals of Friendship, Bradford, Davis, Morse, and Jameson.

It was Governor William Bradford's great-grandson Joshua Bradford who brought his family circa 1748 from Kingston in Plymouth Colony to Meduncook Plantation, where he settled on Bradford's Point, a small settlement that had started five years earlier.

Cornelius Bradford, Joshua's son (born 1737), married Patience Davis, the daughter of one of the founding families in Meduncook. Although Cornelius was accused of "inclining to toryism," we find that he served his country during the Revolutionary War as a captain commanding the 6th Company of Colonel Mason Wheatin's Lincoln County Regiment.[1]

Joshua Bradford Jr., born on April 2, 1746, was just a youngster at the time of the Indian attack when he and his brother Benjamin were captured and carried off to Canada. Picture the trials Joshua faced during the long, arduous trek north into unfamiliar territory, forced to steal from the white settlers by his captors. Survivor that he was, he was able to escape and make his way back home to Meduncook.[2]

Toward the end of the century, Joshua Jr. married Martha Jameson

Melissa Hensel stands next to the Cornelius Bradford house in the mid-1950s.

Photo by James C. Hensel

April 26, 1773 and built her a home on a lovely salt-water farm on Cook's Point (now known as Wadsworth Point in East Friendship). Nothing remains of that original home; fire and the ravages of time

The Cornelius Bradford house in 1862. *Photo courtesy of the Hensel family*

have claimed it. It was a symbol of the character of the early pioneers who faced adversity yet moved on.

Today, nestled on the brow of the hill, stands the quaint home built in 1820 by Joshua Jr.'s son, Cornelius Bradford (born 1788), a homestead constructed of bricks baked on the shores of Cook's Point. You might question its importance. You might not even give it a second glance. Nothing about its exterior indicates its historic value. We often, mistakenly, base our opinions on a home's outward appearance, façade, architecture, or landscaping. The determining factor of its true greatness comes from the character of those who lived there.

Let's take a walk along the shore on Cook's Point where Cornelius set up a brick oven. Examine the rich clay, let it ooze between your fingers, imagine you were there when Cornelius burned brick in the nearby pasture for the house that still stands. Picture his persistent energy as he mixed clay and water to the proper consistency. Consider the skill necessary to mold those bricks and the patience necessary to wait for enough to dry to build his home. Energy, skill, and patience were qualities of the man's character. Each generation builds on the skills, courage, and determination of the past at the same time contributing its own special attributes. It's all real! It's a part of our heritage! It happened!

In Dr. Hahn's *History of Friendship* we read that the children of Cornelius " who built the brick house" went out West. Searching on the Internet, we find Allen Alexander Bradford, born in Friendship in 1815, who made quite a name for himself. After studying law under Jonathan Cilley in Thomaston, he left this area to go to Missouri where he became a member of the Missouri bar and clerk of the circuit court.

Next, he became judge for the Sixth District Court of Iowa. Moving on to Nebraska, he was a member of the Nebraska Territorial House of Representatives. His next move was to Central City, Colorado, where he was appointed by President Lincoln as a judge to the Supreme Court, Colorado Territory, in 1862. He was elected to the U.S. House of representatives 1865-71. His spent his remaining years he in Pueblo, Colorado, practicing law.[3]

Cornelius's sister, Nancy, born in the old homestead in 1780, married Nathaniel Wotton. The Bradford lineage is carried on through Nancy's daughter, Sarah, who married Fred B. Morse. Their daughter, Sarah, married Randall Davis, who lived on a nearby farm. Long had he admired the homestead as a symbol of the staunch New England family into which he had married. In 1883 he seized the opportunity to purchase the homestead.

Randall and Sarah's three daughters, Emma, Sadie, and Mary, never married but worked in Boston. As is often true, children move away to find employment but later are drawn back to their family roots. With the same resolve that centuries ago brought Joshua Bradford to Meduncook and with the same determination to return to his native home that the captured son, Joshua, felt in faraway Canada, Sadie and Emma returned to the old homestead.

The industrious sisters led a busy life; Emma tended a flock of sheep and Sadie kept busy with her embroidery, perfectly finished on both sides. Both Emma and Sadie were expert quilters; their album quilt contained over one thousand pieces. Emma's seaside paintings and rural scenes were an important part of the home's décor. The home is vibrant with the energy, skill and patience of the sisters.[4]

In 1949 after the conclusion of WWII, James Hensel, freelance writer and college professor, and Anita, his wife, were searching for a home to settle down in so James could go on with his writing. Discontented with the homes in the South, they headed north and almost determined to settle in Searsport, Maine. En route, they saw the road sign to Friendship and took Route 220 to investigate the home of the Friendship sloop. Taking a wrong

Neighbor Marjorie Russell at the farm in the 1930s. *Photo courtesy of Everett Russell*

The Cornelius Bradford house in 1949. *Photo by James C. Hensel*

turn at the top of Cook's Hill, they ended up near a home on Wadsworth Point where a caretaker of a home was burning furniture, lovely old Hitchcock chairs. They stopped to question him and offered to buy the furniture. Their offer was rejected, but they managed to get the name of the homeowner. Contacting her, they bought not only the furniture but also the house, a house with no electricity, no plumbing, no telephone. The house became a place of peace, quiet, and solitude, an atmosphere perfect for James to settle into and to get back to writing.

One of the first tasks the Hensels took on in restoring the home was to carefully remove the lovely, wide floorboards, establish a firm foundation for them, and return them to their original location. They spent the next 12 years in Friendship, writing, making friends, taking pleasure in gardening, clamming on the shore, going lobstering with Harold Jameson, raising blueberries, picnicking, and having lobster bakes. Becoming an active member of the community, James participated as a member of the school board.

Keeping this home on Cook's Point, James reluctantly, moved to Worcester, Massachusetts, to become a college professor. Stephen and Melissa, their children, learned to love the home when they summered there and were drawn back to the old Bradford house.

Stephen was able to contact Mary Wiley, whose family had owned the home, and asked Kathy MacLeod to videotape Mary's visit back to the homestead. This special memory capsule was a birthday gift for Melissa Hensel Schacterle, the present owner of the Bradford house.

Known for his special skill in carving realistic birds, Stephen is mak-

ing a name for himself in the art world. In October 2006 the *Lewiston Sun Journal* newspaper reported on the display of his work at the new Auburn (Maine) Public Library as follows: "A great horned owl, an osprey in flight, and a pair of pileated woodpeckers have all found homes at the Auburn Public Library through the efforts of Maine artisan Stephen Hensel, an award-winning woodcarver who began his trade at the age of six. Hensel carved the birds from natural basswood and wood from a linden tree, and brought them to life using expertly applied acrylic paints."[5]

Peregrine falcon bird sculpture by Stephen Hensel. *Photo by Mary Ann Hensel*

Stephen has served as a selectman of the town of Friendship and was a member of the Friendship planning board. He encouraged new residents to "be involved, become a part of the community", a community with 'pioneer roots.'"[6]

Pencil drawing of the back of the Cornelius Bradford house in 2006 by Celia Rose Hensel.

VIII On the Road to Lawry

LAWRY FRIENDSHIP ME. 33.

Photo courtesy Penobscot Marine Museum

39 *The McFarland and Parsons Homes* By Lynn Meyer and Carolyn Foster

On the Waldoboro Road as you come into Friendship sit two little old capes, side by side among homes that are newer and more randomly placed. If you were curious about such things, you would have to wonder about the lives lived in these two old sisters in the days when the road was a dirt path to Waldoboro—and how those lives may have touched upon each other and intertwined as the town grew around them.

The house closest to Friendship is today owned by Judy McFarland Cotton, but records in the Friendship library show that it originally belonged to Cornelius Morton. The name Cornelius Morton is mentioned often in the *Records of Meduncook Plantation*. Genealogy of the Lawry family reveals there have been as many as four Cornelius Mortons before 1800.[1] The Cornelius Morton we are interested in seems to have been born around 1794. *Records of Meduncook Plantation*, indicate that he married two widows; first, the widow of Samuel Lawry III, who died at sea in 1805,[2] and then in 1838, the widow of Captain Oliver Morse.

Lawry descendents have identified Cornelius in the 1810 census as a 10- to 16-year-old, living with the widow Sarah Morton Lawry and three children under 10 years of age. Since Meduncook records show that he had married Sarah Lawry in 1808 (at age 14), he was apparently not of an age to be considered a head of household in the 1810 census.

The McFarland house in April 2007.

Photo by Victor Motyka

McFarland homestead, mid to late 1800s.

Photo courtesy of Arthur K. McFarland, Jr.

McFarland home, circa early 1900s.

Photo courtesy of Arthur K. McFarland, Jr.

The 1820 census, however, shows Cornelius as head of household, living with a woman of between the ages of 25-26, probably Sarah.

In 1826 when 75 acres of the original Lawry land (now Flood's Cove) was sold to Seward Poland II, Cornelius was named as grantor among the Samuel Lawry heirs (in stead of Sarah, the widow) along with Rachel Lawry's husband, Simon Parker, Samuel IV, and Polly Lawry.[3] Not mentioned among those grantors, Samuel and Sarah's son, James, a sea captain, appears to have retained 25 of the original 100 acres, marrying Seward's daughter Martha Poland in 1828 and eventually moving back into the Lawry homestead.[4] Although Sarah was still alive in 1834, when she and Cornelius granted land to Samuel Lawry (IV)[5], she died some time after that, and it is presumably then that Cornelius left the Lawry homestead and James and family moved back.

In 1832 Captain Oliver Morse died at sea,[6] and in 1838 Cornelius and widow Nancy Pitcher Morse announced their intentions. Although Oliver Morse was from a different side of the Morse family, Cornelius's marriage to Nancy Morse may have moved him into the area surrounded by a relative, Jonah Morse. Land inherited and later sold by Oliver Morse's minor son in 1847 is bounded by the Goose River and includes 130 acres, so it seems as if the Oliver Morse family may have been living in the general vicinity before his death.[7]

In 1840 Cornelius Morton was granted land of Samuel Lawry and George Condon[8] (sounds like McFarland property). Abutters at various times included Malachi Delano, who was married to Jonah's daughters (first to Nancy Morse and later to Mary Ann) and whose land was toward Goose River, and an E. (Elijah?) Morse, who had lands toward Cooks Corner.

The Morse connection intensified in 1843 when Cornelius Morton and Nancy Morse Morton transferred the Morton/McFarland property to Samuel Brown, who was married to Jonah's other daughter, Maria.[9] The Morton property stayed in the Brown family till the death of Annie Brown in 1932.

The second house (the one closer to Waldoboro, now owned by Jim and Louise Bowen) was once the old James Parsons homestead, and is said to have been built between 1810 and 1820. James Parsons and Jane Davis were born in 1817 and married about 1839. Wotton family lore remembers Capt. James Parsons and Zenas Cook II as great friends. This appears to be about the time of the Civil War, when Zenas Cook II and Isaac Morse (another brother to Maria and son of Jonah) formed a large boat-building firm; in 1856 they built the schooner *Isaac Morse* for Captain Parsons.

James and Jane Parsons had a son, Lawry Parsons, who married Caroline Flinton in 1865. When James died in 1888, he bequeathed his land holdings in Friendship to his three grandchildren: Herbert received the Lawry farm on Martin Point; Mildred, who married Charles A. Morse, the Parker farm; and Hattie Mabel, who married Alason E. Wotton in 1889, inherited the Parson family homestead.[10] In 1895 Hattie M. Wotton sold the Parson property to Jonah Morse II.[11] He was son of Jonah, the brother to Maria, Isaac, and the father to the illustrious Wilbur A., Jonah D., et al. When Jonah Morse II died in 1904, his heirs sold the Parson homestead to Clayton Oliver. With Wilbur as executor, the signatures on that deed read like the

The Parsons home in winter 2007.

Photo by Lynn Meyer

Carrie Mae McFarland circa 1920s.

Photo courtesy of Christine Wotton Macdonald

who's who of the Friendship boat building aristocracy: Wilbur A. Morse, Sylvester Morse, Charles A. Morse, Jonah D. Morse, Elijah A. Morse, Laura Prior, Mary McLain, Letha Simmons, Albion Morse, Eudora Miller, Amanda Thomas, Mary M. Morse, Sarah J. Morse, Carrie H. Morse, Mildred P. Morse, Elliot Prior, Robert McLain, and Austin Simmons.[12] With those children and in-laws, Jonah II had spawned the Friendship sloop, if not the Friendship fleet.

Hattie Wotton's husband, Alason, had a sister, Carrie H. Wotton, who married Arthur Kelleran from Warren. When Kelleran died three years later, Carrie married Jonah D. Morse, who raised her infant daughter, Carrie Mae Kelleran, along with his own daughter, Bess. Jonah D. was the son of Jonah Morse II and the brother of Wilbur A. Morse. Like his boat building brothers, Jonah D. went on to have his own successful boat building business, moving to Damariscotta in 1924. In Damariscotta his bookkeeper, C. Waldo McFarland, courted and married Jonah's daughter, Bess. Not to be outdone, his stepdaughter, Carrie Mae Kelleran, married Waldo's twin brother, C. Wardell McFarland! When Jonah D. died in 1932, it was his son-in-law Waldo who disposed of his Damariscotta shipyard. Carrie and Wardell McFarland moved back to Friendship, where they bought the other house (Morton/Brown house) from the Annie Brown estate in 1933. The house has been in the McFarland family since that time.

Both households have in recent times made their contributions to Friendship history and heritage, in retelling Friendship's extraordinary seagoing past and conveying the story of the legendary Friendship sloop. Carrie Kelleran served as curator at the Friendship museum for many years, while her daughter-in-law, Phyllis McFarland, collected history as Friendship town librarian. Next door, Llewellyn Oliver, Clayton's son, was someone whose interest in local history and families has helped keep memories intact for many of us. Llewellyn, who died in 1986 at the age of 82, would have been very pleased to see this beautiful book.

Llewellyn grew up in Friendship, where he had many family ties. He recalled listening as a child to his mother and her friends as they talked

Arthur and Phyllis McFarland circa 1987.

Photo courtesy of McFarland family collection

Wilbur Morse Friendship sloop at the current site of Thomas G. Simmons's property. Left to right: Elmus Morse, Clayton Oliver, and Willie Pottle; standing far right is Charles Morse.

Photo courtesy of Arlene Stetson

Gertrude and Clayton Oliver's 50th anniversary celebration.

Photo courtesy of Arlene Stetson

about family and events past and present. After training at Farmington Normal School, he taught briefly in Friendship, including the last term at the Brick School House before it closed in 1922.[13] He taught in a number of Maine communities and spent 14 years as the schoolmaster on Monhegan before retiring to his family home in 1964.[14]

In the summers he returned to Friendship; he was active in local organizations and continued his interest in local history. By 1967, he was contributing periodic columns to the *Rockland Courier-Gazette* under the logo of the Friendship Museum, a practice he continued for the rest of his life. He drew from his own knowledge and from Dr. William Hahn's notebooks on Friendship history. Some of these columns are in collections held by the Friendship Museum and the Friendship library.

One of Llewellyn's stories is worth contemplating at this time as we celebrate the incorporation of "…the plantation called Meduncook… into a Town by the name of Friendship." He told that the origin of the name had to do with the fact that pirates operated in these waters at an earlier time. As a result, it was the custom of local mariners to identify themselves as "friend ship." In other words, they used the phrase as a password that meant, "We are not pirates."

McFarland homestead circa 1950s.
Photo courtesy of Arthur K. McFarland, Jr.

Given the incentive for towns to choose names with positive, promising images which Earle Shettleworth describes so well, and with Harmony, Unity and Hope already taken, Friendship surely must have felt right.

**

Phyllis and Arthur's son, Art, e-mailed from Memphis, Tennessee, with some poignant memories of growing up in the little white house in the forties and fifties:

The side door of the McFarland house in 2006.
Photo by Linda S. DeRosa

"We were what would now be called an extended family, back then we were just family–we lived in the house with Grampie Mac and Grammie Mac (C. Wardell and Carrie Mae Kelleran McFarland). The house was open, but there was their part and our part of the house. At Christmas time Grampie and the boys (Freddy and I) would go into the woods and cut two trees, a big one for us and a small one for Grammie. Ours would be decorated by everyone, but no one was allowed to decorate Grammie's but Grammie. Christmas morning, Fred, Judy, and I would get up early, before the folks, to see what Santa had brought. Later in the day we would open presents under Grammie's tree."

The second remembrance was of storytelling:

"We, the three children, would often gather at night by mother's bed. She would weave tales about boys and girls from another time and place. Grampie Mac also would come to our room and tell stories of tall ships and of pranks that he and his boyhood friends used to play on one another. …This I think is the essence of what was lost."

When questioned about use of the house as a stage stop, and rumors of Indian attacks, Art responded:

"As to the question regarding the house as a stage stop, Grammie and Grampie always referred to the mail carrier as the "stage." Frequently folks would pay the mail carrier to take them to and from Waldoboro. That included at times Gramp, Freddie, and me. I also was told that the house was once used as a sort of rooming house, perhaps in connection with a stage stop. I even remember it being said that Andrew Carnegie's son stayed there. Where fact ends and fable begins is anyone's guess. I dare not even go into the stories of Indian attacks…I think that there are both bricks and casket boards in the walls. I think they would be in the north wall…I do remember that perhaps Indians were said to have attacked from that direction. Truly, I think that the builder used whatever he had in hand, as I know that there are fieldstones, cut stones, and bricks as well as wood in the foundation walls."

The McFarland house in the 1960s.   *Photo by Carlton Simmons, courtesy of Friendship Library*

40 *The Delano Homestead* By Eliza Soeth and Marguerite C. Sylvester

Big house, little house, back house, barn is how Beatrice Delano Wotton referred to her family homestead on top of the hill in Lawry, Friendship, Maine. This charming farmhouse in rural, coastal Maine has a rich history dating back to 1770 when the first Delano moved to Friendship. Andrew Wyeth was once seen in the field studying the homestead. What a beautiful Wyeth painting it would make.

Christopher Newhouse, a German from Boston, acquired the property circa 1770 and built a small cape. Christopher moved here from Waldoboro with his wife, Margaret Sides (Sitz), widow of Loring Sides Sr., who was killed in Waldoboro by Indians in 1757 during the French and Indian Wars.[1] Her daughter, Margaret (Peggy Sides), married Alpheus Delano on April 26, 1770. Alpheus Delano was born on October 2, 1744, in Duxburgh, Plymouth, Massachusetts. His ancestors had been in Plymouth since 1621, when 19-year-old Philippe De la Noye arrived at the Plymouth Colony from Leyden, The Netherlands aboard the *Fortune*.[2] Over the next century, the name De la Noye was gradually changed to Delano.

Alpheus Delano had come to the Meduncook (Friendship) area to check out his father Judah's land purchase in Back Cove. Judah had purchased Jones Neck at Broad Bay for 110 pounds from Samuel Waldo Jr. Previous to this, Alpheus had been a soldier for the British in the French and Indian Wars and had been a prisoner of war. After marrying Peggy

Tommy Delano homestead in 1998.

Photo courtesy of the collection of Eliza Soeth

Three of Thomas Delano's daughters in front of the homestead, circa late 1800s.

Photo courtesy of the Wotton family

Sides, Alpheus and his wife settled here on the land of his in-laws and started a family. Their first son, Nathan, was born on January 18, 1771, and at least seven more children would follow over the years.

Alpheus joined the revolution and fought for the freedom of America in the Revolutionary War. After the war, on the 14th of February 1786, Alpheus purchased 150 acres from his father-in-law, Christopher Newhouse. He "paid two hundred pounds lawful money" for land abutting the east side of the Goose River. Here began Friendship's first generation of Delanos.

Alpheus became involved in town affairs and would frequently buy and sell property. He served varying terms as town clerk, tax assessor, and surveyor of roads. In 1807 he was one of six original members of the old Congregational Church in Broad Bay, Waldoboro. He lived with his son Judah and was listed as head of household on the 1790, 1800, 1810, and 1820 censuses. In 1820 Alpheus applied for pension for services in the American Revolution. In the application he stated that his property consisted of two cows, four sheep, and old household furniture. Alpheus died March 9, 1826, in Friendship. His gravesite is unknown.

Over the years, Alpheus sold parcels of his land to his sons Nathan and Judah. The house passed on to Judah who built the small house into a full cape, circa 1809-1810. He married Judith Weed of Thomaston, a minister's daughter, in 1810. He and Judith would have 12 children there. Judah held a license to sell liquor in 1812. It is known that the post-and-beam cape was built before the War of 1812, as the width of the floorboards in some parts of the house are over 12 inches, which was outlawed during wartime. Judah used pegs to construct the beam roof of the post-and-beam cape.

In 1865 Judah left the property to his son Malachi. Malachi lived on Bremen Long Island and decided to deed the house to his brother

Thomas and his wife, Diantha, who would raise 14 children here. He was a prosperous fisherman. After the Civil War, Thomas remodeled the house. He removed the center chimney, enlarged the doors and windows, and added the old Lawry schoolhouse (formerly the Wolfgrover blacksmith shop) as his new kitchen.

After the death of Thomas in 1904, the property passed to his son William, who would become the fifth generation to own the land. William was also a fisherman. In 1907 he built a great three-story barn, one of the largest in Friendship, at a cost of $700. The foundation was made of granite. The barn still stands today, strong and tall with straight lines. William housed animals in the barn and pigs in the basement. The old two-seater outhouse is still in the barn as is the hatch door to the basement piggery. There was a carriage house built on the back north side of the barn; it has fallen and all that remains is a partial foundation. There is a very large rhubarb plant behind the barn, and William told his granddaughter Beatrice (Delano Wotton) that the plant was there when he was a child in the 1860s. This plant still thrives, making it over 150 years old. It has been divided many times and shared with local folks.

William married Lola Simmons and had one son, Warren Thomas "Tommy" Delano. After William retired from fishing, he had a candy and soda store in the northeast front of his home where an orchard now stands. Beatrice said he would fall asleep in the afternoon and the local kids would come by and steal small bits of candy.

Warren Thomas "Tommy" Delano was born in 1904. He inherited the property from his father, William. Tommy married Ethel Benner in 1921. They had three children, Beatrice, Gerald, and Reginald. Tommy was a fisherman and well-loved character about town. He is well remembered by many today. His wife, Ethel, served as a mail lady for many years. Tommy fished from Benner Island and Friendship. In the winters he worked at Scott Carter's boat yard. During World War II, he was the

Front view of the Tommy Delano home with creeping Jenny and lobelia in summer 2002.

Photo by Eliza Soeth

foreman of the Waldoboro shipyard. Tommy and Ethel enjoyed dancing and went to the dances in South Waldoboro almost every weekend. He was an avid hunter, especially of fox hunting, and he had his own hounds, Walker hounds. His shop on the wharf was a great place for working and socializing. He was a past member of the Freemasons' Meduncook Lodge.

Tommy was very superstitious—no blue on the boat, no pig on the boat, and hatch covers never upside down.[3] He was very proud of his barn and of the fact that it only cost $700 when it was built in 1907.

After Tommy's death in 1989, his remaining child, Beatrice Delano Wotton, inherited her beloved childhood home. She would be the seventh generation to own the home. As Tommy grew older, the home slowly fell into need of repairs. None of Beatrice's family was interested in restoring the house. She rented it for a short time, and the house continued to decline. She sold the property to a restoration company in 1998.

In the fall of 1999, Scott Nelson and his wife, Eliza Soeth, moved to Maine from Sun Valley, Idaho. They were searching for property in the Midcoast when they visited the Delano homestead, which was then partially restored and listed on the real estate market. They immediately fell in love with the land and the look of the classic New England home and barn. They purchased the home in March 2000. They worked on the floors, sanding away years of varnish. In the kitchen they removed old linoleum, discovering beautiful birch floorboards, which Beatrice had never seen. The rooms were all painted in replica colonial colors. Antique style light fixtures were installed throughout the home. The Nelsons tried to finish and decorate the home in a colonial style.

The unique features in the home include the pegged beams in the upstairs bedroom, the schoolhouse walls in the kitchen, and the footprints in the borning room floor. Standing next to the window in the borning room, now her office, Eliza noticed two footprints were worn into the old wide pine floorboards. After all, at least 38 children are known to have been born here. That is a lot of baby rocking, standing, and looking out the window. It is a good thing.

Scott and Eliza are proud stewards of this land and respect and enjoy its rich history and people. Eliza began a variety of gardens in 2000. She and Scott installed a long raised bed, colonial style vegetable garden. She surrounded her garden with espaliered apples and pears as were done at Mount Vernon and Monticello. She planted an orchard, a large berry garden, and numerous perennial flowerbeds. Scott built many arbors for her many vines. There are also hedges of lilacs, roses, and alleys of crabapples and linden. The land has become a mini arboretum. They garden about two acres of the five-acre homestead, which is all that is left of the original property. Amidst all the digging, many bottles, buttons, marbles, crockery, and odds and ends have been discovered in the rich soil. Many large maple trees were preserved on the edge of the woods, and a very large ash tree still stands at the back of the barn. The woods have been thinned, and lovely trails have been carved to meander through the beautiful woods of maple, oak, birch, ash, and pine. It is a joy to stroll through the moss and around the great old stones. Eliza sells cut flowers, perennials, and photographs in the summer from her flower stand, The Lavender Rose Garden.

The Nelsons feel extremely privileged and honored to have known the late Beatrice Delano Wotton, the last of the seven generations to live in the homestead. She passed away in 2005. Beatrice was a good friend and so welcome in the home. She loved coming in and sitting at the old kitchen table and telling stories of her childhood. Her eyes would light up and she would glow with delight as she reminisced about her mother and father and her two brothers. It was a home filled with love and good times. Beatrice referred to the kitchen as the "little house," as it was once the old Lawry schoolhouse. The building was the Wolfgrover blacksmith shop before it was a school, and it may date back to the late 1700s. There are carvings and writings on the walls of the wainscoting in the old kitchen, tales of early school life in Friendship. The present owners discovered this writing after removing very old wallpaper. These walls really *do* talk!

Delano homestead barn with onions drying in fall 2001.
Photo by Eliza Soeth

Delano homestead with delphiniums in summer 2006.
Photo by Eliza Soeth

IX The Friendship Museum

George Huey merganser decoy. *Photo by Linda S. DeRosa*

Photo by Linda S. DeRosa

41 *The Brick Schoolhouse* By Marguerite C. Sylvester

Down through the years, from the time of the first school in Meduncook Plantation in 1759 when Levi Morse was the teacher until today's Friendship Village School with its dedicated teachers, there have been many schools in Friendship. Although each has had its individual stories, our thoughts center on the Brick Schoolhouse.

In the 1800s schools were constructed of wood so they could be moved to accommodate the larger number of pupils. It was quite apparent, in days gone by, that the gentleman with the most influence would move the school close to his family. Occasionally a school might be moved secretly with a team of oxen in the dead of night. Such actions tended to cause the building to become very rickety.

Deciding that this condition was a matter of concern, William Condon of Hatchet Cove and Edmund Wotton of Goose River called a meeting of the differing factions to solve the problem. The decision was to build a centrally located building, a building constructed of brick to insure its permanence. The result was the little red brick schoolhouse with a projecting woodshed along the front serving as a vestibule and entry. With four blackboards and desks for twenty-five pupils, school opened in 1851. Hannah Oram Condon was the first teacher at an outrageous salary (many thought it was too much pay) of one dollar a week.

Ken Murphy relates his story of attending this one-room schoolhouse: "It was called Hatchet Cove School and was made of brick

The Brick Schoolhouse in summer 2004.

Photo by Linda S. DeRosa

except for the backhouse, which was wood and shingled. The total school population was about eighteen, and this covered eight grades, plus one teacher who taught all subjects. We took turns arriving early on cold mornings to start a fire in the pot-bellied stove near the front of the room. We took turns visiting a nearby farm, usually my grandfather's, to bring a bucket of fresh cold water from the well. With the use of a dipper and small collapsible cups, we could quench our thirst comfortably.

"The furniture, as was true in all those one-room buildings, consisted of a table for the teacher with one of those tap bells to get our attention plus about twenty desks and chairs for the kids. Let us not forget the bench down front where we all had to go when we had a lesson or when we recited. The blackboards were ordinary wood boards painted with black paint, which always made the chalk squeak when any writing or figuring was done.

"Little did I realize that the same Hatchet Cove School had been attended by a famous educator from Friendship. He was my mother's first cousin, Dr. Randall Condon. He ended his career as superintendent of schools in Cincinnati, Ohio." [1]

The last term of the school with Llewellyn Oliver as teacher was in 1923. Dr. Condon purchased the building in 1927 and restored it in memory of his mother, Hannah Condon. The ownership passed on to his grandson, Randall Foster.

Randall J. Condon's " The Kindergartner's Creed" hangs on the wall, a memento of the children who entered the doors of the Hatchet Cove School. A portion of it follows:

THE KINDERGARTNER'S CREED

"I Believe in little children as the most precious gift of heaven to earth. I Believe that they have immortal souls, created in the image of God, coming forth from Him and to return to Him

"I Believe that in every child are infinite possibilities for good or evil and that the kind of influence with which he is surrounded in early childhood largely determines whether or not that budding life shall bloom in fragrance and beauty, with the fruit there of a noble Godlike Character.

"I Believe it to be the mission of the kindergarten to
Step by step
Lift bad to good
Without halting, without rest
Lifting better up to best." [2]

In 1965 a group of twenty-five citizens, recognizing the need of a home to preserve the history of the town and its artifacts of the early days, met and formed the Friendship Museum Organization. The following officers were elected: President, Albert Roberts; Vice-president, Randall Foster; Treasurer, Robert Lash; and Secretary, Mary Carlson. Dr. Frank Foster leased the so-called Red Brick Schoolhouse where one of his ancestors had been the first teacher. [3]

Watercolor by Clint Lawry in the collection of the Friendship Museum.

Photo by Linda S. DeRosa

The Brick Schoolhouse in the mid-1880s.

Photo collection of Friendship Museum

Once it was established that the school would be a suitable site for the display of memorabilia that gave a clear picture of life in the community of Friendship, Carrie McFarland was hired as curator. Those genuinely interested in the history of the town and the nautically minded who were seeking the origin of sloops, draggers and the old way of fishing soon found a wealth of information to share

Here was a half-hull of a lobster boat; beside it was a half-hull of a Friendship sloop; adjacent to it was a picture of the original builder, Wilbur Morse; in one display was a picture of George Huey, a nationally famous decoy carver; in another corner, a picture of teacher Ralph Wincapaw and pupils attending school at that time. Soon there was a plethora of items, dishes, tools, toys, all revealing life in the early 1900s.

One can easily be filled with nostalgia by studying Clint Lawry's painting of the S. S. *Monhegan* with Captain I.E. Archibald at the wheel at the "siding" at Jameson and Wotton's wharf, taking on passengers for her run between Rockland and Portland. Each arrival and departure became a community event.

Years have passed since that important informational meeting of the Friendship Museum. Interest fluctuated over the years, but under the leadership of Lynn Case and her ever-available and supportive husband, Bill Case, many improvements have been made. It became quite evident with the immensity of the number of items to be displayed that there was a need for more adequate display cases. A more efficient cataloguing system was developed. Attention was centered upon the importance of preserving and caring for the many items with archival methods. Lighting was improved, walls painted, floors resurfaced, and the exterior of the building was renovated. These improvements, plus an enlarged parking area and better landscaping, gave birth to a renewed interest in the museum's programs. In July 2001 the museum building was donated to the Friendship Museum, Inc. by Randall and Sally Foster in memory of Hannah Yates Condon and Dr. Frank C. and Katherine C. Foster.

Because of the wealth of artifacts available, interesting and informative displays are rotated each year. One display was about The Lobster Conservancy, an organization interested in the preservation of the lobster industry, the town's main livelihood. Another featured the granite quarry on Friendship Long Island, an industry in the early 1900s. One year great interest was shown in the book, *The Amanda Letters*, centering on letters sent to a local Friendship girl during the Civil War period. The book gave insight into life during that time and revealed how the war affected Friendship.

In recent years retired schoolteacher Sally Merrick, representing the Museum, has collaborated with sixth-grade teacher Gaylea Hynd, to develop the oral history project called "Finding Friendship." The sixth graders, along with their teacher, select a topic and then tape oral interviews with individuals related to that subject. In their first project, "Schools Past and Present," pupils interviewed citizens about changes in schooling. The next year, as many of the students were already hauling their own lobster traps, great excitement was created as they interviewed local fishermen for "Lobstering, a Friendship Tradition." For the third project, "Answering the Call to Duty," students interviewed Friendship's veterans from World War II up through Desert Storm. In the 2006 project, "Working in Friendship," students researched the different types of businesses conducted in the community in the early 1900s.

Students happily anticipate taking part in the next project. Sally Merrick and Gaylea Hynd as well as the students deserve much credit and thanks for the effort they have made recording much of our history.[4]

Enjoy your visit to the Brick Schoolhouse. Explore the many valuable stories within its walls preserving the history of Friendship.

Sally Merrick lectures at the museum for the Thomaston Senior College on the "Finding Friendship" oral history project in September 2004.   *Photo by Linda S. DeRosa*

Friendship Museum in summer 2006.   *Photo by Linda S. DeRosa*

Addendum

Sunday dawn at Friendship harbor.

Photo by Fran Richardson

The Sterling-Morton Farm By David Henderson

The farm had been in my family until 1943, when Everett Russell bought it from my great-great grandparents, Bert and Ella Morton. It had actually been Ella's family's farm since it was built. They were Sterlings, probably from Monhegan. Bert ran the farm and was a lobster buyer in Friendship.

I grew up listening to my grandmother Irene Morton Henderson tell stories about life in Friendship in horse and buggy days. I think it was her way of staying connected to Friendship after my grandfather Randolph Henderson moved his family to New Bedford, Massachusetts, to pursue his photography aspirations. My grandmother grew up living in Friendship village above Morton's store, which later became Jameson's market, but any time she had the chance, she stayed with her grandparents at the farm in East Friendship. Gramp (Bert) built her a log cabin on top of the hill behind the house. She always spoke of being able to see Monhegan in those days, when the hill was all blueberries, before the spruces grew up. She remembered playing with Penobscot Indian children whose families camped down on the river behind the

The Sterling-Morton house in April 2007.

Photo by Paul Mahoney

farm in the summer. They wove baskets here, which they sold to tourists. I have found a few small baskets in the house that I assume came from those local Indians.

On one of the kitchen windowpanes, scratched in perfect penmanship is the name Sarah Morton. My great-aunt, Sally Foster, her daughter, theorizes that her mother was "testing" her diamond!

Everett Russell made few changes when he bought the place in 1943. He continued to farm, rake blueberries, and cut pulpwood.

Sarah Morton "tests her diamond" on the kitchen window in the farm circa 1930.
Photo by Paul Mahoney

Around 1956 he built a house for his sister, Marjorie, on the north end of the field on the same side of the road as the farmhouse.

In the 1980s Everett began putting up the windmills that power his machine shop. His first was on the roof of the shed across the road from the house. Later he built two on freestanding towers behind the shed. One still operates.

My partner, Paul Mahoney, and I bought the place from Everett in June 2001 when Everett moved into his sister's house after her death. He's a great resource to us with his farming

We believe these baskets were made by the Penobscot Indians who set up camp seasonally on the Friendship River.
Photo by Paul Mahoney

Bert and Ella Morton with friends and lambs in 1930.

Photo courtesy of the Morton family collection

knowledge of the place and his plain old Yankee ingenuity. We've learned so much from our neighbors, especially Everett, who seems to know a little bit about everything. Renovating the house has been a real neighborhood effort. Neighbors Steve Cobb, Carl Mueller, Victor Motyka, and Peter Bulkeley have played important roles in this work. Paul's pottery studio wouldn't have been built without their help.

Painting the weathered clapboards was bittersweet. In exchange for longevity, some of the house's rustic beauty was lost.

Indian woman and child who camped on the Friendship River seasonally.

Photo courtesy of the Morton family collection

Having the farm back in the family was my childhood dream. Living and working here, painting and making pottery, renovating the house, raising sheep and gardening, we feel connected to my forebears who worked and lived on this farm.

The Morton family reunion in 1931, held at the cabin on the high hill behind the homestead that Bert Morton built for his granddaughter Irene Morton Henderson. *Photo courtesy of the Morton family collection*

Everett Russell's working windmill in April 2007.

Photo by Paul Mahoney

Sterling-Morton farm, circa 2001.

Photo by Paul Mahoney

The Johnson house in winter 2006

Photo by Elaine Lang Cornett

The Johnson House
by Cicely Aikman Scherer

The Johnson house, dark grey with cream trim on 34 windows plus
Two picture windows gazing out at the world
Perched on a steep knoll looking out to sea
Looking out to Cushing and Monhegan Island
A pathway dipping down to Friendship harbor,
On a May morning in 1972 we fell in love with you.
Apple blossoms tumbling down the hill
Two great blues flying across the horizon,
As we looked out from the porch the deal was sealed,
Though you said don't tell the real estate agent
How much we like this house.
Flowers on the wallpaper
Light flowing in the windows from all directions
How could we resist 33 years ago?
A path pitched 45 degrees down, leading to the cove
Water over our heads at high tide

A mud flat hiding clams at low
The changing tides, the paths of sun and moon
Revealing our pulsating world.
One hundred years ago this house was a summer hotel.
Boats sailed up from Boston
Letting passengers off at the big rock.
They hiked up to the house to stay a week or two,
Evenings, Japanese lanterns decorated the lawn and they danced.
In front a huge oak tree was planted as a slip in 1902,
Its trunk now measures 83" in circumference
Its branches protect the front of the house
Hides flying squirrels, spreading acorns on the lawn.
We spent 31 years here through the lives of three dogs and seven cats
Through blizzards, heat waves, rainbows, terrifying thunderstorms
Surprises of mackerel, lobster feasts, blueberry pancakes, dandelion wine
A place of Heaven on earth.

Photo by Elaine Lang Cornett

The Attic Speaks

The Homes of Friendship
At the harbor, the village, or on a point,
In East Friendship, Finntown or Lawry,
Homes extending their Welcome!
Homes hoarding cherished memories,
Homes abounding with tranquillity and love.
Homes rejoicing over the birth of a child,
Homes echoing happy children's voices.
Homes mourning the death of a loved one,
Homes that have weathered the storms of life.
These are the homes of Friendship.

Prized mementos hidden in the attic,
In a trunk, dusty and aged, under the eaves;
Protecting treasured memories,
Lasting evidences of past joys.
A bundle of letters declaring undying love,
A daughter's fragile wedding gown,
Grandmother's patchwork quilt,
A child's prized doll and a teddy bear,
Here a diary of years gone by.
Secure in the attics of the homes of Friendship.

Marguerite C. Sylvester

Epilogue

Schooner *Alice S. Wentworth*

Photo by Chub Patch from the Friendship library collection

May the ocean greet you as a friend
May the wind be soft upon your face
May the red sun at night be your delight
May all ships you meet be friend ships,
And until we meet again
May all storms be hushed until you are safe
In Friendship harbor.

by

Linda S. DeRosa

Notes

CHAPTER 1: FRANKLIN ISLAND LIGHT

1. Stephen H. Burns, interview, Friendship, Me., February 2007.
2. Dr. Hahn's notes at Friendship Library.
3. Albert James Clinch, Historical notes from grandson, Terry L. Clinch.

CHAPTER 2: CAPTAIN JAMES SIMMONS HOUSE

1. *Chronicles of Cushing & Friendship* (Rockland: Maine Home Journal, 1892), p. 65.
2. Ivan Morse, *Friendship Long Island* (Middletown: Whitlock Press, 1974), p. 85.
3. Ibid, p. 88.
4. Ibid, p. 93.
5. Co-Curators: Arlene Barnard and Sam Cady, *The Arts of Friendship* (Rockport: Maine Coast Artists, 1999), p. 12.
6. Photographs by Jed Devine, Letter by Jim Dinsmore, *Friendship* (Gardiner: Tilbury House, 1994), p. 41.

CHAPTER 3: OLIVER MORSE HOUSE

1. Carleton W. Morse, *Island Heritage 1974*, Trigilio Family Collection.

CHAPTER 4: INTRODUCTION TO FLOATING HOMES

1. C. William Vogel, *History of Friendship, Maine* (Orono: University of Maine, 1957), pp. 15-16.

CHAPTER 5: MELVIN SIMMONS HOUSE

1. Mildred Reed, interview, Friendship, Me., July 2006.
2. Bradley Beckett, "Nothing Fazed Lottie," *Yankee Magazine*, December 1998, p. 22.

CHAPTER 6: MELVIN SIMMONS STORE

1. Charles B. McLane, *Islands of the Mid-Maine Coast* (Gardiner: Tilbury House, 1992), pp. 159-160.

CHAPTER 7: CHUB PATCH HOUSE

1. William Hahn, *History of Friendship* (Friendship: Self-published), pp.1-4.
2. Captain Bob Lash and Bill Jameson discussion, cassette tape, Friendship, Maine Library, 1967.
3. Betty Roberts, Friendship Sloop Days Yearbook, "Island Hopping," 1962, p. 22.

CHAPTER 8: INTRODUCTION: *"THE CORNER"*

1. William Hahn, *History of Friendship* (Friendship: Self-published), section titled: "Friendship Businesses Through the Years," p. 3.
2. Llewellyn H. Oliver Notebook, Friendship Library Collection, compiled from William Hahn's notes.
3. Eleanor Winchenbach Diary, Gordon Winchenbach's Collection.
4. William Hahn, *History of Friendship*, section titled: "Friendship Schools," p. 2.

CHAPTER 9: ZENAS COOK II HOUSE

1. Melville B. Cook, ed., *Records of Meduncook Plantation and Friendship, Maine 1762-1899* (Rockland: Shore Village Historical Society,1985), pp. xi-xii.
2. Ibid.p. xii.
3. William Hahn, *History of Friendship*, Friendship: Self-published), section titled, "Francis Shipwreck," pp. 1-2.

CHAPTER 10: CAPTAIN WILLIAM JAMESON FARM

1. E. O. Jameson, *The Jamesons in American, 1647-1901*, (Boston: 1901).
2. Jameson Family History from the collection of Patricia Jameson Havener.
3. E.O. Jamesons, *The Jamesons in America,1647-1901*, (Boston:1901).
4. Ibid.
5. Courtney MacLachlan, T*he Amanda Letters*, (Bowie, Heritage Books Inc., 2003).

CHAPTER 11: NELSON THOMPSON HOUSE

1. Dr. William Hahn papers at Friendship Public Library.
2. *Vogue Extravaganza* Special Fall Issue 2006.
3. Dr. William Hahn papers at Friendship Public Library.
4. William Hahn, *History of Friendship*, (Friendship: Self-published).
5. Newspaper clipping at Friendship Public Library.
6. Les Thompson ledger at Friendship Public Library.
7. Friendship Day Records.
8. Bruce Wallace, interview, Friendship, Me., September 2006.

CHAPTER 12: WEBB THOMPSON HOUSE

1. Dr. Hahn's Notes at Friendship Library, pp. 49-52.
2. Ivan Morse, *Friendship Long Island*, (Middletown, Whitlock Press, 1974), p. 133.
3. Author's personal recollection of Charlie Murphy.
4. Friendsip Sloop Races of 1965, pp 33-36.
5. Phyllis Austin, newspaper article, 3/2/1971.
6. Neil Lash, interview, Friendship, Me., December 2006.
7. Eldon E. Libby, Shell News 1971.
8. Kurt and Amy McCollett, interview, Friendship, Me., November 2006.
9. William Hahn, History of Friendship (Friendship: Self-published), section titled: "Lash Family Genealogy."

CHAPTER 13: KITT JAMESON HOUSE

1. E. O. Jameson, *The Jamesons in America, 1947-1901*, (Boston, 1901).
2. Courtney MacLachlan, *Amanda Letters* (Bowie: Heritage Books, 2003), p. 77.
3. Pat Jameson Havener's family papers.
4. Pat Jameson Havener, interview, Friendship, Me., November 2006.
5. Ellen Jameson, oral history.
6. Ibid.

CHAPTER 14: NELLIE DAVIS HOUSE

1. A Friendship Museum news piece by Llewellyn Oliver, date of publication unknown.
2. Notes left by Dr. William Hahn (revered and beloved physician, who was also an avid student of local history, late of Friendship) that were later annotated and updated by Llewellyn Oliver.
3. Friendship Museum news piece, Llewellyn Oliver.
4. Courtney MacLachlan, *The Amanda Letters* (Bowie: Heritage Books, 2003), pp. 3,144.
5. Davis Family records provided by Patricia Jameson Havener.
6. Records provided by Kathy MacLeod at the Friendship Town Office.
7. An Old English term, a smack is a vessel fitted with seawater flushed well or a dry well, which is used to transport fish to market. In Maine, lobster smacks have been in use since the early 19th century, carrying live lobsters between ports in Maine and the Maritimes, Boston and New York.
8. A copy of the obituary announcing the death of Elijah Davis, circa Dec. 1916, publication unknown.
9. Beth Delano, *Stone Reunions: A comprehensive look at the cemeteries of Friendship, Maine* (Camden: Penobscot Press, 2005), p. 91.
10. Except for the teaching position in Conway Center, New Hampshire, all of the schools at which Nellie taught were in towns within Maine.
11. It is assumed that this amount is paid per week.
12. Two or three years prior to her death, Nellie fell at her home, breaking her hip. The accident rendered her unable to walk again, and she entered the Fieldcrest Nursing Home in Waldoboro where she stayed for the rest of her life.
13. A conversation with Ann Alvis and Larry Jennings.
14. Records provided by Kathy MacLeod at the Friendship Town Office.
15. Conversation with Ann Alvis and Larry Jennings.

CHAPTER 15: THOMAS BENNER HOUSE

1. Herbert Benner, conversation.
2. Ibid.
3. Ibid.
4. Ibid.
5. *Lewiston Evening Journal*, November 11, 1922.

CHAPTER 16: WALTER H. WOTTON HOUSE

1. *Portland Sunday Telegram & Sunday Press Herald* 1927, May 8, 1927, Section A, p. 4.

CHAPTER 17: SHERMAN TECUMSEH JAMESON HOUSE

1. Jameson family history from the collection of Patricia Jameson.
2. Ibid.
3. Ibid.

CHAPTER 18. THE DAVIS HOUSES

1. William Hahn, *History or Friendship* (Friendship: Self-published), section titled: "History of Friendship," pp. 1-4.
2. Eaton Davis, interviews, Friendship, Me., 1999-2001.
3. Courtney MacLachlan, *The Amanda Letters* (Bowie: Heritage Books Inc., 2003).
4. Melville B. Cook, ed., *Records of Meduncook Plantation and Friendship, Maine 1762-1899* (Rockland: Shore Village Historical Society,1985), Appendix II, "Rebel in Maine Waters," pp. 118-119.
5. Letha Rasmussen, interview, Friendship, Me., August 2006.

CHAPTER 20: JAMESON & WOTTON WHARF

1. Allison M. Watts, "When the Boat Came In" (Friendship: Friendship Museum Collection).

CHAPTER 21: BURT MURPHY HOUSE

1. Note from William F. Redmond to Alan R. Bellhouse, 1990 (quoting unknown source).
2. This cottage is now owned by the Spear family, and is known as "The hotel."
3. Bellhouse family converstions, 1969-1984; conversation with Marguerite C. Sylvester 2007.
4. Conversations with Alma L. Black, 2006 and 2007.
5. Conversations with Alan R. Bellhouse, 1962-1985. Period photos of the properties on the end of Davis Point indicate that many of the Murphy-built stone walls at the Spruces were already in existence before the 1920s, so this stone wall might have been laid as part of the last wall, or perhaps it was laid as part of a repair.

CHAPTER 22: THE GENERAL ELLIS SPEAR COTTAGE

1. Abbott Spear, ed., *The Civil War Reflections of General Ellis Spear* (Orono: University of Maine Press, 1997).
2. Arlington National Cemetery Website, www.arlingtoncemetery.net/espear.htm.
3. Priscilla Ambrose, *Cottages of Davis Point, 1835-2000* (Friendship: 2001).

CHAPTER 23: WILBUR MORSE HOUSE

1. William Hahn, *History of Friendship* compiled by Mary Carlson (Rockland: Good Impressions 1988), section titled: "Boats Built at the Morse Boat Shop in Friendship," pp. 2-4.
2. Lew Dietz, *Night Train at Wiscasset Station* (New York:1977), pp. 137-141.
3. Ibid.
4. Ibid.
5. Letha Rasmussen, interview, Friendship, Maine, August 2006.
6. Herald Jones, ed., *It's a Friendship* (Seth Low Press: 1965), p. 48.
7. Al Roberts, ed., *Enduring Friendships* (International Marine Publishing Co., 1970 #71).

CHAPTER 24: EDWARD THOMAS JR. HOUSE

1. William Hahn, House Histories - collection of private papers; envelope # 4, Friendship Public Library.
2. Thomas C. Hubka, *Big House, Little House, Back House, Barn*, (Hanover: University Press of New England, 1984) pp. 5-6.
3. William Hahn, *History of Friendship*, compiled by Mary Carlson (Rockland: Good Impressions, 1988), p. 3.
4. Ibid. p.3
5. Ibid, (no page number) section titled, "Friendship Town Roads."
6. Ibid, section titled, "Boats Built at the Morse Boat Shop in Friendship," p. 2.
7. Knox County Registry of Deeds; Knox County Courthouse, Rockland: Book 288, p. 63.
8. Jed Devine and Jim Dinsmore, *Friendship* (Gardiner:Tilbury House, 1994), p. 2.
9. Joe McHugh, *The Flying Santa* (Nevada City: Calling Crane, 2002) p. 8.
10. William and Maude Olsen, interview, South Bristol, Me., September 2006.

CHAPTER 25: THE THOMAS FARM

1. Melville B. Cook, ed., *Records of Meduncook Plantation and Friendship, Maine, 1762-1899* (Rockland: Shore Village Historical Society, 1985).
2. Collection of Robert Lash, Jr.

CHAPTER 28: FRED YOUNG HOUSE

1. Charles B. McLane, *Island of the Mid-Maine Coast*, Vol. III (Gardiner: Tilbury House, 1992) p. 107.
2. Bradford Young, interview, Friendship, Me., Fall 2006.
3. Phillipe Von Hemert, interview, Friendship, Me., Summer 2006.

CHAPTER 30: KERR EBY HOUSE

1. Knox County Registry of Deeds, Book 7, p.132.
2. Ibid.
3. Melville B. Cook, ed., *Records of Meduncook Plantation and Friendship, Maine 1762-1899* (Rockland: Shore Village Historical Society,1985), p. xi
4. A.E. Sutton, *The Lawry Family of Friendship, Maine 1754-1982* (Camden: Penobscot Press, 1992), p. 8.
5. Christine Wotton Macdonald, interview, Warren, Me., March 2007
6. Cook, *Records of Meduncook Plantation*, p. 27.
7. Ibid. p. 76.
8. Ibid. p. 84.
9. Marlene A. Groves, CG, *Vital Records of Friendship, Maine* (Rockport: Picton Press, 2004), p. 20.
10. Knox County Registry of Deeds, Book 16, p. 258.
11. Naval Historical Center, http://www.history.navy.mil/ac/artist/e/eby/eby1.htm.
12. *The Norwalk Hour*, May 30, 1936.
13. Celeste Prime, interview, Friendship, Me., August 2006.

CHAPTER 31: JAMES & HANNAH CONDON HOME

1. A. E. Sutton, *The Lawry Family of Friendship, Maine 1754-1982* (Camden:Penobscot Press, 1992), p. 81.
2. William Hahn, *History of Friendship,* Mary Carlson, compiler (Rockland: Good Impressions, 1988), p. 48.
3. Ibid., p. 20, p. 97.
4. Ibid., p. 48.
5. Ibid., p. 48.
6. Ibid., p. 48 and personal communication from Maynard Condon to Carolyn Foster, circa 1970.
7. Interview with Stanley Lawry by Carolyn Foster, 1980.
8. Ibid.
9. Unpublished records of the Friendship Village Society and The Roadside Cemetery Association.

CHAPTER 32: SAMUEL LAWRY HOUSE

1. A.E. Sutton, The Lawry Family of Friendship, Maine 1754-1982 (Camden: Penobscot Press, 1992), pp. xiii, 40.
2. Ibid., p. xiii.
3. Ibid., p. 40.
4. Ibid., p. 43.
5. Ibid., p. 42.
6. Ibid., p. 33.
7. Clinton Lawry, Jr., interview, Friendship, Me., Summer 2006.
8. Marjorie Lewis, interview, Friendship, Me., Summer 2006.

CHAPTER 33: CAP'N AM'S HOUSE

1. Edward Poland Jr., telephone interview, Round Pond, Me., October 2006.

CHAPTER 36: ZEBULON DAVIS HOUSE

1. Knox County Registry of Deeds, Knox County Courthouse, Rockland: Book 23, p. 392.

CHAPTER 37: HJALMAR AUTIO FARM

1. Ahti Autio, interview, Friendship, Me., 2006.
2. Friendship Senior Citizens, *Celebrating the 1900s in Friendship* (Friendship:Self-published, 1999), recollections of Vieno Autio.
3. Arnold Autio, interview, Friendship, Me., 2006.
4. Robert Armstrong, interview, Friendship, Me., 2006.
5. Sue Armstrong, interview, Friendship, Me., 2006.
6. Nancy Penniman, interview, Friendship, Me., 2006.

CHAPTER 38: CORNELIUS BRADFORD HOUSE

1. Melville B. Cook, ed., *Records of Meduncook Plantation and Friendship, Maine 1762-1899* (Rockland: Shore Village Historical Society, 1985), p. 17.
2. *Sunday Telegram,* 9/14, special dispatch.
3. Biographical Directory of the United States Congress.
4. Stephen Hensel, interview, Friendship, Me., 2006.
5. *Lewiston Sun Journal,* newspaper article, October 1, 2006.
6. *Friendship Folks* Video, Volume 1.

CHAPTER 39: MCFARLAND & PARSONS HOMES

1. A. E. Sutton, *The Lawry Family of Friendship, Maine 1754-1982* (Camden: Penobscot Press, 1992), pp. 195-196.
2. Ibid. p. 110.
3. Knox County Registry of Deeds, Book 143, p. 163.
4. Sutton, p. 132.
5. Knox County Registry of Deeds, Book 4, p. 400.
6. Beth Delano, *Stone Reunions* (Camden, Maine: Penobscot Press, 2005), p. 50.
7. Lincoln County Probate Records, Oliver Morse.
8. Knox County Registry of Deeds, Book 4, p. 458.
9. Knox County Registry or Deeds, Book 11, p. 459.
10. Knox County Probate Records, James Parsons.
11. Knox County Registry of Deeds, Book 104, p. 268.
12. Knox County Registry of Deeds Book 129, p. 292.
13. *Courier-Gazette*, March 25, 1982, p. 2.
14. William Hahn, *History of Friendship*, compiled by Mary Carlson (Rockland: Good Impressions, 1988), p. 20.

CHAPTER 40: THE DELANO HOMESTEAD

1. Jasper Stahl, *History of Old Broad Bay and Waldoboro* (Portland: The Bond Wheelwright Company, 1956), pp. 213-214.
2. Nathaniel Philbrick, *Mayflower* (New York: Penguin Group, Inc., 2006), p. 125.
3. Information gleaned from interviews with Wotton family members: Blake, Lance, Craig, and Betty Wotton and Sharon Wotton Brazier, Friendship, Me., Summer 2006.

CHAPTER 41: THE FRIENDSHIP MUSEUM

1. Ken Murphy, *Me* (Friendship: Self-published, 1991).
2. Portion of Randall Condon's *The Kindergartener's Creed* on display at the Friendship Museum.
3. *Courier-Gazette* Newspaper article.
4. Marguerite C. Sylvester, *Friendship Museum Coastal Locker*, Back Yard Yacht Builder's Internet Magazine, 2005.

Sunset at Bradford Point

Photo by Fran Richardson

Bibliography

Ambrose, Priscilla. *Cottages of Davis Point, 1835-2000*. Friendship, Me.: 2001.

Barnard, Arlene, and Sam Cady. *The Arts of Friendship*. Rockport, Me.: Maine Coast Artist, 1999.

Beckett, Bradley. *Nothing Fazed Lottie*. Yankee Magazine, Dec. 1998.

Chronicles of Cushing & Friendship. Rockland, Me.: Maine Home Journal, 1892.

Cook, Melville B., ed. *Records of Meduncook Plantation and Friendship, Maine, 1762-1899*. Rockport, Me.: Picton Press, 2004.

Delano, Beth. *Stone Reunions*. Camden, Me.: Penobscot Press, 2005.

Devine, Jed and Jim Dinsmore. *Friendship*. Gardiner, Me.: Tilbury House, 1994.

Dietz, Lew. *Night Train at Wiscasset Station*. New York, N.Y.: Doubleday, 1977.

Duncan, Roger F., et.al., Al Roberts, ed. *Enduring Friendship*. Camden, Me.: International Marine, 1970.

Eby, Kerr. *War*. New Haven, Ct.: Yale University Press, 1936.

Friendship Senior Citizens. *Celebrating the 1900's in Friendship*. Friendship, Me.. Self-published, 1999.

Groves, Marlene A., compiled & ed. *Vital Records of Friendship, Maine, Prior to the Year 1892*. Rockport, Me.: Picton Press. 2004.

Hahn, Dr. William. *History of Friendship*. Compiled by Mary Carlson. Friendship, Me.: Self-published.

Jameson, E. O. *The Jamesons in America, 1647-1901*. Boston, Ma.: 1901.

Jones, Herald, ed. *It's a Friendship*. Rockland, Me.: Seth Low Press, 1965.

Kearney, Harold and Marie. *Martin Point*. Friendship, Me.: Self-published, 1986.

MacLaclan, Courtney. *The Amanda Letters*. Bowie, Md.: Heritage Books, 2003.

McHugh, Joe. *The Flying Santa*. Nevada City, Ca.: Calling Crane, 2002.

McLane, Charles B. *Islands of the Mid-Maine Coast, Volume 3*. Gardiner, Me.: Tilbury House and The Island Institute, Rockland, Me: 1992.

Morse, Carleton W. *Island Heritage*. Friendship, Me.: Self-published, 1974. Trigilio Family Collection.

Morse, Ivan. *Friendship Long Island*. Middletown, N.Y.: Whitlock Press, 1974.

Murphy, Ken. *Me, an Autobiography*. Friendship, Me.: Self-published, 1991.

Philbrick, Nathaniel. *Mayflower*. New York, N.Y.: Penguin Group, 2006.

Roberts, Al, ed. *Enduring Friendships*. Camden, Me.: International Marine, 1970.

Roberts, Betty. Friendship Sloop Days Yearbook. *"Island Hopping,"* 1962.

Stahl, Jasper. *History of Old Broad Bay and Waldoboro*. Portland, Me.: The Bond Wheelwright Co., 1956.

Sutton, A.E. *The Lawry Family of Friendship, Maine, 1754-1982*. Camden, Me.: The Bond Wheelwright Co., 1956.

Sylvester, Marguerite C. *Friendship Museum Coastal Locker*. Back Yard Yacht Builders, Gaff Rig Internet Magazine, 2005.

Vogel, C. William. *History of Friendship*. Orono, Me.: University of Maine, 1957.

Woodward, Colin. *The Lobster Coast*. New York, N.Y.: Viking, 2004.

Lorraine Lash with Elise and Emma at the end of Bradford Point in summer 2006.

Photo by Fran Richardson

Index

Rock wall at Bradford Point

Photo by Fran Richardson

Photo by Fran Richardson

Friendship sign at Goose River made by the late Carl Mueller, selectman and community leader.

Photo by Paul Mahoney

Friendship Homes: If These Houses Could Talk, was produced by Custom Museum Publishing in Rockland, Maine. Founded in 2005, Custom Museum Publishing offers affordable solutions for the printing and publishing needs of small museums, historical societies, galleries and individual self-publishing writers and artists. The company specializes in full-color, high-end, digital printing and graphic design of cards, posters, gallery guides and perfect bound exhibit catalogs and historical books. Custom Museum Publishing uses the newest printing technology to make printing and publishing affordable, even in small quantities.

Custom
Museum
Publishing

www.custommuseumpublishing.com

in Rockland and Portland, Maine 207.594.0090 | email: info@custommuseumpublishing.com

479 Main Street, Suite 201
Rockland, Maine 04841

141 Preble Street, 2nd Floor
Portland, Maine 04101